URBAN
EVANGELISM

Biblical-sociological Principles to Reach the Cities

URBAN
EVANGELISM

Biblical-sociological Principles to Reach the Cities.

MANUEL A. ROSARIO

Original Title:

De la iglesia a la calle

Consejos prácticos para un evangelismo urbano eficaz.

Author:

Manuel A. Rosario

Published by:

CreateSpace, an Amazon company - 2014

Charleston, SC,USA

Translated by:

Anne Elise Machado

Text Edition:

Enrique González

Cover design and layout:

Víctor Campusano

Dedication

To our Lord Jesus Christ - author and finisher of our faith - in whose life, death, resurrection and priesthood, the gospel takes hold.

Acknowledgements

I am deeply grateful to God for inspiring me to write about such an exciting subject; thanks also to my wife, children, parents, siblings and friends, for their support during the process.

Author

Manuel A. Rosario, PhD, is a passionate about the science of salvation. He is also the director of Evangelism of Greater NY Conference of SDA. His experience as a metropolitan pastor and his academic formation permits him to discuss the topic from distinct angles. He is married to psychologist Jazmín Tolentino, with whom he has fathered two children: Carlos Manuel and Carolin Jazmín. He is the author of the book *Mayordomía es Salvación*, published by the Interamerican Publishing House.

Table of Contents

Introduction

WE OFTEN HEAR of the urban: Sociology, psychology, geography and even urban music! We are in a new cultural explosion, with new models of behavior, attitudes and forms of coexistence, which are evident in urban citizens.

The rural-urban dichotomy, was raised by European economists, philosophers, sociologists, and psychologists in the nineteenth century, who differentiated between city singularities to those of the country; by 1903, the German scholar Georg Simmel raised in his essay, *The Metropolis and Mental Life*, that the stresses to which the citizen was exposed to, gave shape to an agitated and nervous personality type.[1]

Horacio Capel summarizes the central ideas of Simmel's work using the words, "Life is more intellectual in a large city." Furthermore, in the cities the pace of life is faster than in the small towns in the countryside and in the country, and there is an "intensification of a nervous life." The multitude of excitations that occur determine whether someone is unable to react to them and lead to man-weary, product type from the big city. The attitude of citizens toward their neighbors is of caution, but the city offers a freedom that is not found in any other place, although this is linked to loneliness...[2]

What an enlightened vision! Wouldn't you say? Two decades later, the sociologist, Max Weber defined the city as a new type of community and later, investigators from the Chicago school wrote in their articles about urban sociology, published during the 1920s in the American Journal of Sociology, that it was responsible for creating new forms of behavior.[3] Shocking! Wouldn't you agree?

Similarly Ortega and Gasset, in his book *The Revolt of the Masses*, first published in 1929, explained:

> "The cities are full of people. The houses full of tenants. The hotels full of guests. Trains full of passengers. The cafes full of customers. The streets full of pedestrians. The famous medical wards full of patients. The shows full of spectators. The beaches full of bathers. What once used to be no problem begins to be almost continuously: finding space."[4]

Although several decades have passed and the effect of the masses has increased, paradoxically, the citizen confesses to be increasingly isolated. The apathy of great urban centers, the hyper individualism and syndrome of the lonely crowd, are direct sources of depression and suicide. The city is the place of those who have no place, where voluntary marginalization is the standard.

Social networks are trying to fill the void; the connection has grown, but not the strong commitments. Sadly, the person to person contact has given way to mask to mask contact. People need people, not machines, real company! And it is not about meeting people, but people who empathize, and this is precisely what is missing in the cities.[5] Today more than ever are the words of Christ true: "Do you not say, 'Four months more and then the harvest'? I tell you, open your eyes and look at the fields! They are ripe for harvest."[6] Here is a great opportunity for the gospel!

Cities and Evangelism

For the 1970s, evangelists, administrators and Adventist theologians, especially in the United States, showed great concern for the apparent impact of city effect on evangelism, which is why in the General Conference Session of 1980 held in Dallas, a secularism committee was appointed under the direction of Dr. Humberto Rasi, in order to understand the phenomenon and find strategies to address it.

The same expectation was appreciated among Catholics, who in 1979 under the leadership of the Latin American Episcopal Council (CELAM), gathered their bishops of Latin America and the Caribbean, to study the new evangelization that, in their view, America and the world needed. As reactions to the insisting Second Vatican Council (1962 - 1965) where it was repeatedly proclaimed, "humanity is experiencing a new period of history."[7] And to the subsequent insistence of Paul VI, who pointed as one of the new social problems the urban phenomenon, in his Apostolic Letter *Octogesima Adveniens*, from May 14 1971.

Again in October 1992, during the celebration of the V Centenary of American Evangelization, held in Santo Domingo, D. R., the need for a new evangelization was argued, defining it as the set of actions to place the gospel in active dialogue with the modern and the postmodern. The world had entered a new phase and the church should adopt a new form of evangelization, articulated in new methods, new expressions and a new fervor.[8]

Alister McGrath, professor of historic theology at the Oxford University, and director of Wycliffe Hall[9], says that Christians were negligent due to the immediate rise in church attendance after the Second World War. For most congregations, evangelism had lost all sense of urgency when they believed all people would come anyway.

He continues: "And then came the crisis of the 60s. *Time Magazine* published the following headline, "Is God Dead?" Secularization had deeply affected western society... In the 70's the large churches started losing their members at a disturbing rate. By the end of the 80's a pattern was identified. Churches committed to outreach were still growing, but the ones not committed were shrinking.[10]

The American Religious Identification Survey of 2008 documented the dramatic decline. In just one generation the American adults who declared themselves christians dropped from 86% in 1990 to 76% in 2008! In a historic decrease of 10%. On the other hand the growing segment that shows non religious preference: atheists or agnostics rose from 8.2% in 1990 to 14.1% in 2000 and then to 15% in 2008.[11]

It is surprising that different groups coincide in pointing out the secularization phenomenon in the new urban context as the challenging element of evangelization; and it is sad to think about what one of the scholars who concluded the Adventist study, Doctor Paulien, said, that the document did not have the desired impact due to it being considered highly technical.[12]

You may ask yourself, what does all this have to do with preaching the gospel? Quite a lot! The gospel is eternal, but societies are ever changing, for this reason it is so dangerous to attempt to change the message as well as not wanting to update the methods. Peter and Paul served the same gospel in different packaging; they knew very well that it was not strategic to follow the same method to evangelize Jews and Gentiles.

To some extent the effect of secularization on evangelism is very similar to the progression of cancer in the human body, silent but sure. We can deceive ourselves and consider that our mission fields are protected, but that's how some North-American Adventist congregations of the 50's, which do not exist today, felt.

The truth is that those who were born or lived part of their lives in the country and then migrated to the cities or were caught by them, are dying and giving way to a new generation that is unfamiliar to the countryside. Consider the challenges multiple churches are facing trying to keep the second and third generation of Adventists. We must look ourselves in this mirror at the local level. If we pray and take steps then the results could be different. "A prudent man sees danger and takes refuge, but the simple keep going and suffer for it."[13] Secularism has been capable of changing great churches into museums.

Urban evangelism, biblical-sociological principles to reach the cities, is intended to serve as a stimulus for the study of the subject. Jesus loves the cities; He cried over Jerusalem, cries over our cities and seeks workers who will cry like Him. The question still resounds: Whom shall I send and who will go for us?[14]

This book is composed of 15 chapters distributed into five sections, described below:

The first section, composed of chapters one and two, is called: *The Metropolitan Context*, and aims to provide an overview of the rapid development of cities and the type of modern citizens who dwell in them or will be very soon. It is discussed how the social facts affect evangelization and what we can do to be more effective in urban preaching.

The second section, composed of chapters three to five, is called: *Urban Mission* and it rekindles the sense of mission of the remnant people. It also outlines the distinctive features of the biblical prophets and draws an analogy between the prophetic mission of John the Baptist and the Seventh-day Adventist Church, and it also dedicates a space to analyze the implications of the third angel's message in the context of urban evangelization.

The third section, composed of chapters six to eight, is called: *The Enemies of Urban Evangelization,* and warns of the major internal enemies that the church faces in the fulfillment of its mission: apathy, prejudice, and evangelistic discrimination, as well as the biblical guidelines to address them.

The fourth section, composed of chapters nine to thirteen, is called: *The Challenges of Urban Evangelization* and raises the need to utilize the scientific and technological tools available in building the kingdom of God, which among other things includes some ideas on how to gather relevant information from the community and integrates it into a practical strategic plan to potentialize local evangelistic work. This section examines the role of the media in evangelization as well as small groups ministry and other evangelistic methods, of no less relevance. It also considers the urgency of increasing the role of youth and children in the advancement of the everlasting gospel, as well as defining structured plans to reach the middle and high classes, and special groups.

The fifth and final section, composed of chapters fourteen and fifteen, is called: *The Success of Urban Evangelism,* and focuses on the need that our houses of worship are perceived to be real cities of refuge, shelters of love and peace. The section also analyzes some of God's wonderful promises to fund his work and it highlights the Holy Spirit as the Missionary Leader by excellence of the church.

I hope that this book will be a great blessing in your spiritual life; that it contributes to the community in which you live in, and that it inspires a new evangelizing air in the church in which you assemble together and serve.

As John L. Dybdahl well said: "Mission is central to our identity; Jesus did not create the church and then gave her a mission as one of her responsibilities. The divine plan of salvation precedes the church. Mission gave birth to church, it is her mother. The very essence and nature of the church is missionary. If the church stops being missional, she has not only failed in one of her responsibilities, she also ceases being the church and becomes only a social organization with religious orientation."[15]

Manuel A. Rosario

The Metropolitan Context

This section aims to provide an overview of the rapid development of cities and the type of modern citizens who dwell in them or will be very soon. It is discussed how the social facts affect evangelization and what we can do to be more effective in urban preaching.

Chapter 1

A Look at the Cities

On October 31, 2011, symbolically, humanity met the milestone of seven billion people, of which an increasing proportion lives in cities. It is expected that by June 15, 2025 the world will have reached eight billion people, and by June 18, 2083 an astronomical ten billion earthlings.[1] At the rate we are going it seems impossible to fulfill the Gospel mandate: "And this gospel of the kingdom will be preached in the whole world as a testimony to all nations, and then the end will come."[2]

Actually, it is not only about the demographic explosion, it is equally necessary to consider the unprecedented growth of urban areas. In mid-2009, the number of residents in the urban fringes (3.42 billion) for the first time exceeded the inhabitants of rural areas (3.41 billion) making the world more urban than rural. It is expected that this global level of urbanization surpasses from 50 percent in 2009 to 69 percent in 2050.[3]

Although the concept of city is not a consensus issue in sociology, the European Conference of Statistics in Prague defines it as an agglomeration of more than 2,000 inhabitants whose population engaged in agriculture does not exceed twenty-five percent. They also consider that from 10,000 inhabitants, all urban agglomerations are cities, if they are concentrated and are primarily engaged in industry, commerce or services.[4]

For other experts it is sufficient to indicate that a city is an urban entity with high population density which is dominated mainly by manufacturing and services, what matters is the level of development in relation to the territory in which it stands.[5]

The numerical criterion alone is not a proof.[6] They also discard the rural-urban opposition, at least in the highly industrialized countries, and consider the increasing impact of intermediate levels, as suburban or semi-urban areas outside the metropolis with fast access to them, which are especially attractive to the middle and high strata.

The truth is that many urban centers are expanding rapidly, transforming villages into towns and then into cities and megacities. Historically, urbanization is driven by the concentration of investment and employment. It is estimated that 80% of global gross domestic product is generated in urban areas, which consequently attracts more capital, more labor force and more people.[7]

The United Nations, aware of this reality, concluded stating that the next two billion people of world population will live in the cities; therefore it is very important to start planning for them now.[8]

I wonder, is it not also a good tip for the Seventh-day Adventist Church? The world today is urban, and it is necessary that the church takes this into consideration as we budget our priorities and determine our concerns. This new scenario presupposes a theological reflection about the cities and the future of urban life.[9]

Mega and meta cities

One aspect to consider carefully in the context of urban evangelism is of the megacities or metropolis with a population of over ten million people. It is risky to refer statistics around large cities, because it will be outdated in a short time, but according to the World Urbanization Prospectus: 2014 Revision, the ten most populated cities in the world in descending order are:

1. Tokyo in Japan,
2. Delhi in India,
3. Shangai in China,
4. Mexico City in Mexico,

5. São Paulo in Brazil,

6. Mumbai (Bombay) in India,

7. Kinki in Osaka

8. Beijing in China

9. New York-Newark in the U.S.,

10. Al-Qahirah in Cairo.[10]

It is convenient to refer that the official statistical projections of the UN in its vision to 2025 does not indicate significant changes in this list.[11] It is appropriate to note that even though the Asian continent is at the forefront in the emergence of megacities, in general the percentage of urbanism by geographical area is as follows: North America 82%; Latin America and the Caribbean 80%; Europe 73%; Africa 40%; Asia 48%.[12]

This data in no way represents a contradiction since megacities are also a political theme of financial globalization.[13] Sociologist Rudi Maier stated, "The massive numerical growth does not represent a reality all the time". On the contrary, as Manuel Castells describes, its strength lays on the meaning of global economy. The mega cities cannot be seen just by their numerical size, but also for their importance on global scenario.[14] We must admit that an urban person is a global person!

A similar theory to that of Maier is supported by Sir Peter Hall, professor of urban planning and urban trends expert at the University of London. In fact, as in the days of the Tower of Babel, crowds are a symbol of power. The strategic plan of Babel was to place man in the sky. [15]

In the case of the cities ranked above, each has a population of over thirteen million inhabitants, highlighting Tokyo as the largest urban agglomeration in the world, with over thirty-six million. It should be noted that cities with a population of over twenty million people are name Metacities or hyper cities, Delhi and São Paulo also fall in this range. It is expected that by 2025 Mumbai, Dakar, Mexico City, New York-Newark, Kolkata and Shanghai will have been added to this elite group.

The megalopolis

If the phenomenon of large cities is surprising, what can we say about the union of many urban centers or megalopolis, a term introduced by the geographer Jean Gottman in 1960 which describes an urban *continuum* of hundreds of kilometers and a population of more than twenty million people, that makes contact with the area of influence of another city and so on. These large urban extensions are characteristic of developed countries, particularly the United States, Japan and Western Europe.[16]

Among the major megalopolis distinguished in global scale is BosWash extending from Boston to Washington, including metropolitan areas like New York, Philadelphia and Baltimore. It brings together a population of approximately 50 million people and is an area of great economic, political, and cultural dynamism. Another famous megalopolis is Tokaido, made up of the Japanese metropolitan areas Tokyo, Yokohama, Nagoya, Osaka and Kobe, with around 45 million inhabitants, forming the most important concentration of economic and technological potential in the world.

Life in the cities

In these urban agglomerations, as mega and meta cities are technically called, live hundreds of thousands of families, crowded into multifamily housing resembling huge honeycombs, which also move in means of transportation where the people feel canned and drowned in a very small space. On the other hand, cities are also centers of economic growth, technological progress and cultural development which make them particularly attractive.

The city is a place of intense contradictions:

"It kills, destroys, and gives heart attacks, cancer and other physical and psychological maladies... It is the place for mobs, gangs, delinquency, drug addiction, and every kind of evil; since long time ago it is the Babylon that corrupts naïve spirits with their youthful ideals [...]. On the other hand the city can also be a place to find answer and resources to solve most of the same problems. It is a place where important decisions are taken, a place for business and jobs.[17]

An author who is impossible to overlook given his significant contributions in this regard is Louis Wirth, German-born American sociologist who in the first half of the twentieth century, specified with unquestionable precision the characteristic features of urban way of life, namely:

- Social isolation;

- Secularization;

- Segmentation of roles;

- Loosely defined standards;

- Social relations characterized by superficiality, anonymity, and transient nature and utilitarian;

- Functional specialization and division of labor;

- Spirit of competition, against the solidarity of rural societies;

- High mobility market economy, dominated by secondary and impersonal relationships over the essential ones;

- Weakening of fragile family structures and

- Disappearance of family relationships with extended relatives.[18]

It seems like a prophecy!

In her time, Ellen G. White commenting on the lifestyle of the cities said:

"The physical surroundings in the cities are often a peril to health. The constant liability to contact with disease, the prevalence of foul air, impure water, impure food, the crowded, dark unhealthful dwellings, are some of the many evils to be met."[19]

In a second statement the said author insists,

"Life in the cities is false and artificial. The intense passion for money getting, the whirl of excitement and pleasure seeking, the thirst for display, the luxury and extravagance, all are forces that, with the great masses of mankind, are turning the mind from life's true purpose. They are opening the door to a thousand evils. Upon the youth they have almost irresistible power."[20]

For *UN – HABITAT* these cities are so huge that they have changed the dynamics of urbanization, making people travel daily from outlying villages or suburbs to work in them.[21] One of the mega cities characteristics is that they have several downtown areas. Places that attract businesses, social and political activities.[22] Usually, these economies are based on advanced production services, especially financial, banking, advertising, legal, administrative assistance and insurance.

These cities and urban belts generate their own rules and impose a new lifestyle that greatly impacts people and consequently changes their habits and character.

The new Red Sea

Reflecting on this phenomenon of urban demographic explosion and considering the mandate to preach the gospel, some questions arise; Did God not consider the exponential growth of humanity by placing such disconcerting objectives for evangelism? Since the completion of the preaching of the gospel is the distinctive sign which marks the second coming, when will the end come?

Fortunately, there are no mistakes with God, as it is written, the gospel will be preached and then shall the end come. The Scriptures state that at the fullness of time Jesus came to the earth for the first time[23] and when the time is fulfilled He will come for the second time. For man it could be an uthopy, but for the God who opened the Red Sea and the Jordan, it is not difficult to fulfill His will once more. Ellen G. White said:

> "Go to work, it is the word of God to you. They cannot see the end from the beginning and yet pray, create and advance. 'Go forward' was the word of the Lord to Israel as they stood with the Red Sea before them and Pharaoh's host pressing hard after them. They obeyed, and as Moses smote the water with his rod, lo, they parted and stood up on one side as a wall, making a path over which the people passed in safety. With faith and trust let us go forward in the word that the Lord has given us, assured that He will be with us as our Helper and Protector.[24]

It seems that the preaching of the gospel is the new Red Sea that must be crossed as we leave Egypt, and the great Jordan which the people of God needs to cross before taking possession of Canaan. Ellen White emphasized:

"The work in the cities is the essential work for this time. When the cities are worked as God would have them, the result will be the setting in operation of a mighty movement such as we have not yet witnessed."[25]

The Lord never asked Moses to open the sea, neither did he demand Joshua to divide the waters of the Jordan; it would be a waste of time. God did the miracle! He just ordered them to go forward. Obedience is the key.[26]

1st Evangelistic Principle

Total obedience

To be a prophetic church means that we will succeed by following the lines traced by God, not our own. It is our turn to march. That is the order!

PRACTICAL IDEAS

1. Find a map of your community and determine the geographic location in which your church is located.

2. Mark on the map the mission field of your church or group of churches.

3. Find out if your area is more urban than rural or more rural than urban.

4. Find out about the official number of people in your community, whether provincial municipality, city, state [...]

5. List the industries that are in your community and think of a plan to evangelize their employees and executives.

6. Correlate the number of people in your region with the number of active members of your church; reflect upon the magnitude of the task and pray to God for strength and courage.

Aim today by the grace of Christ to obey the order to march!

Chapter 2

A Look at the Citizens

When planning the evangelization of our cities, it is essential to first consider those who are or will be soon its undoubted inhabitants, the postmodern citizens. While the most common meaning of postmodernism became popular with the publication in 1979 of the work: *The Postmodern Condition* of Jean-François Lyotard, the term had already been used previously.

In sociology, the term postmodern refers to a cultural process identified mainly in developed countries in the early 70s, but observed in recent decades in different parts of the planet. It is the so-called secular-mind, a phenomenon even more convincing in the United States and Europe, but not exclusive to those latitudes, because secularization occurs in all societies as they become modern.[1]

In his essay, *Urban Mission in a Postmodern World*, Kleber De Oliveira, Ph.D. in missions and director of the Center for Secular and Postmodernists Studies of the Adventist Church, proposes postmodernism as a result of urbanization, and globalization as one of its channels for worldwide broadcast, and in which he states:

> "The centralizing power of urbanization makes urban context the place where postmodern condition occurs. As perceptively noted by Erwin McManus: 'If postmodernism were a painter, his canvas would be the city.'"[2]

The secular mind

The ideology that rules the postmodern man is secularism. A secular person is someone that lives with little or no reference to God or religious practice on a daily basis. Being a secular person usually is not a conscious decision; the majority of secular people are not atheists. The typical secular person may not be hostile towards religion, but is someone that doesn't practice most religious traditions such as reading the Bible, praying or attending worship.[3]

The traditional secular mentality, hedonistic and individualistic, is well represented in the Bible by Esau, the profane who sold his birthright (a spiritual blessing) for a bowl of lentils. The secular cannot discern spiritual things, and makes no distinction between the holy and the profane.[4] Recall that the Apostle Paul warned Timothy that in the last days there would be a generation "lovers of pleasure rather than lovers of God – having a form of godliness but denying its power."[5] Actually, secularism is more than a new phenomenon, it is a rendition of the days of Noah that has been strengthening and mutating throughout generations.[6]

Joao Batista sheds light when he explains:

"The urban world has an extreme secular ideology centered on individual pleasure; and religious motivations lose their strength there. Religion is only attractive if it sparks pleasure and fulfillment. An extreme competition with other forms of pleasure offered by a wide spectrum of city options.[7] The church on the other hand can no longer be a toy or fun center in the city, which follows the principles, strategies, methods and rhythms of the world, on the contrary is the church of the living God, which constantly points to the Lamb of God who takes away the sin of the world."[8]

Evolution of postmodern thought

Dr. Humberto M. Rasi in his essay, *The Challenge of Secularism*, develops the four basic assumptions that have characterized traditional secularism, namely:[9]

- *Contingency:* All that exists is the result of chance in the universe, which has always existed by itself.

- *Autonomy:* Men are independent and only they can determine their own destiny.

- *Relativity:* There is no absolute morality; time and place are the ones that determine what is acceptable for a particular individual or group of people.

- *Timeliness:* Since there is no empirical evidence of life beyond the grave, death is the end of everything.

On the other hand, Dr. Jon Paulien, who has studied the evolution of postmodern culture for decades, raises the coexistence of two very contrasting trends of secularism: the traditional secular and postmodern secular. To understand this is fundamental to the advancement of the gospel in our cities. He argues that, in broad terms, it can be said that the traditional secular mind does not fight God, but He is not present in his or her everyday life. However, in present days, a second trend has made peace with spirituality, giving way to the secular postmodern thought, whose characteristics are clearly visible in the form of conversion of important figures of the media. Nevertheless, biblical faith still cannot conquer a society that is increasingly 'spiritual' but less religious.

The secular postmodern, whose growth has been evident in recent years in religious terms are opposed to traditional secular, in the sense that they are 'very spiritual', take time for private meditation, enjoy contemporary worship and meetings of praise in homes, so long as they are not required to provide a long term commitment. They are aware of God, but establish their own agendas to relate to Him. They are determined to cultivate a private relationship with God for themselves, without religious institutions or moral mandates. They are in charge of their own spiritual life. Their two distinctive characteristics are autonomy and relativity, as well as sharing the hedonistic principles with the traditional seculars. [10]

Psychosocial characteristics

In spite of the two trends previously outlined, it is very difficult to segment the postmoderns because of their high level of independence and social change, yet there are some psychosocial characteristics that they have in common. Here are some of the most relevant for evangelistic purposes:

1. Incredulous about the meta narratives, shutting out the possibility of a story beyond the story[11]

2. Deeply disillusioned, has renounced uthopies and is committed to individual progress.

3. Sensitive to environmental issues and moral values.

4. Compulsive buyer.

5. Values and promotes cultural diversity and the richness of diversity.

6. Has replaced ideology with the image; gives more value to the form and degree of conviction produced than to the content of the message.

7. Downplays the importance and authority of traditional sacred texts.

8. Assumes mass media to be criteria of truth, if it does not appear in mass media it does not exist.

9. Has lost privacy. His/her life and that of others is a show, especially in the context of social networks.

10. Desecrates politics.

11. Demystifies the leaders.

12. Questions the great religions.

13. Searches for the immediate. The future and the past have lost their importance.

14. Turns to the mystical looking for questions and answers.

15. Truth is a matter of perspective or context and not universal.

16. Constantly worried about major disasters and the end of the world.

It is necessary to address that the postmodern man tries to explain and live his or her life from here and now, so it becomes difficult to accept a cosmic explanation to his or her private sorrows.

Although we know from the Word of God that the struggle between good and evil is real, and that there was a war in heaven in which Michael and his angels fought against the dragon, we must be wise in presenting it so that it does not generate unnecessary rejection. A good strategy to teach the great truths of the gospel is one used by Pastor Hermes Tavera in the book "2012 y el Verdadero Fin del Mundo" (*2012 and the True End of the World*). He taps into a media phenomenon to attract attention to biblical truth, and when the postmodern reader comes to realize, he or she is already understanding the great prophecies of the book of Daniel, interpreting the sanctuary, diving into Revelation and wanting to be among the faithful redeemed. As you can see, it is not hiding the truth. Never! But it is using the bait that the people of this generation will bite on.[12]

How to reach the secular mind?

Largely, this book is precisely about this, however I will sprinkle some ideas and will refer to the proposals of two of our best examples, Paulien and Norman Jean Earnan.

Dr. Paulien, based on what he calls the *"evangelism of salt"*, in which you have to mingle with whom you want to reach, outlines nine very interesting steps to work successfully with the secular mind. His thoughts are challenging and pose a real transition and evangelistic revolution at all levels:

1. Moving from public evangelism to relational evangelism.
2. Moving from short term evangelism to long term evangelism.
3. Moving from our own personal agenda to one that is focused on the needs of others.
4. Moving from a church based in the neighborhood to a church that is supported by the workplace.
5. Moving from a single focus or evangelistic style to multiple approaches.
6. Moving from the concentration on baptism to the concentration of the process of salvation.
7. Moving from the building to the community.
8. Moving from the control of the church to the control of God.

9.   Moving from an exclusive evangelism to an inclusive evangelism.

As can be seen, most of these are relational aspects and it is what Michael Green raises as he tries to answer the question, Why are there non-Christians? and propose ideological reasons, reasons of the past, intellectual reasons and reasons of the heart. If we try to bring people to Christianity, but we avoid the challenges that faith poses to the human mind, we will not get lasting results.[13]

A second proposal is presented by Dr. Ernan A. Norman in his book entitled: *A Strategy for Reaching Secular People*, which devotes an entire chapter to submit three proposals of which I will address one: the seven-step strategy used by Willow Creek Community Church in Illinois, which collects the largest quantity of information possible and then create a profile of their prospective worshipers.

They believe that the essence of persuasion is to move a person from where they are to where they should be, and for them this is crucial information.[14] Specifically the proposal is:

- Building authentic relationships with unbelievers with the well-defined idea of taking them to Christ.

- Share personal testimony, for which they receive training.

- Invite new worshipers to a service designed especially for them.

- Set a weekly service with an emphasis on evangelism.

- Integrate new worshipers to a small group.

- Discover and develop the spiritual gifts of new visitors to integrate them into one of the ministries identified by the church.

- Teach the biblical principles of stewardship, teaching the new believers that all they are and have belong to God and they should honor Him returning the tithe, or 10% of all income.[15]

I must say that Dr. Earnan's proposal focuses on planting

what he calls "intentional churches", defined by the author as churches that structure their initiative with the purpose to reach unchurched secular people.[16]

Among the series of steps involved in the proposal are:

- Cultivate the vision,

- Understanding secularization and secularism,

- Raise local information,

- Start advanced strategic planning,

- Ministerial analysis to determine how the church is equipped for the task,

- Establish teams of service according to the gifts,

- Do a demographic study to determine the values,

- Including commitment, establish a biblical mission statement,

- Brief and comprehensive, build the vision statement, indicating what kind of church we want to plant and

- Develop practical and contextualized strategies.[17]

We must also rethink our method, because as Michael Green proposes, the first question people ask is not, "is it right?" but, "what consequences this will bring to me?" It is not enough to know, it is necessary to experience. Pragmatism? Yes. The experts say the climax of the New Age movement is a reaction to the modern spiritual drought of the Enlightenment. The great emphasis that the Enlightenment puts in rationalism became boring and irrelevant.

We can not state that we have the truth anymore, or we will sound like arrogant triumphalists, and calling everybody else liars. In the pluralistic environment where most of us live today, saying that someone has the truth will be seen as intellectual fascism.[18]

This book propose a new advancing strategy: *Christ's method of witnessing!* You will say it is an old method, but I follow the logic of Christ by expressing: 'A new commandment I give you: Love one another as I have loved you, that ye also love one another.'[19]

Although it was old, [20] for them it was brand new. With the secular mindset, today as in the time of Christ social openness precedes spiritual openness.

In due time we will deal with it in more detail, but as a reminder:

> "Christ's method alone will give true success in reaching the people. The Savior mingled with men as one who desired their good. He showed His sympathy for them, ministered to their needs, and won their confidence. Then He bade them, 'Follow me.'" [21]

Go and do the same!

The end of the speech

In his presentation, *The Church in the City*, Joao Batista Libanius argues that although the city is the place of invisible religion, where religion loses its external location and is internalized, these inner realities remain if they are fueled by the conviction, so that religion needs to find times and places to strengthen the conviction, even if it means more effort from pastoral creativity. [22]

The conclusion is obvious; if we want to reach the cities it is necessary that we strive to understand the mentality of the people living in them. With good reason Ellen White said:

> "He who seeks to transform humanity must himself understand humanity. Only through sympathy, faith, and love can men be reached and uplifted." [23]

We must also become familiar with social phenomena such as globalization and its impact on evangelism; we are dealing with postmodern citizens, which, due to urban development and the globalization process, are not confined to a secluded area of the planet, but trapped in the inversion of values and cultural relativism, and are not strangers, but our own family, friends, neighbors and coworkers. We are challenged to learn to deal with the postmodern mind or resign ourselves to look away from the faith, in many cases our own family.

Fortunately victory is assured, since in 1909 Ellen White wrote:

> "I saw jets of light shining from cities and villages, and from the high places and the low places of the earth. God's word was obeyed, and

as a result there were memorials for Him in every city and village. His truth was proclaimed throughout the world."[24]

The postmodern mind cannot prevent Christ from entering into the hearts of the millions who at the last minute will respond to the gospel.

2nd Evangelistic Principle

Understand how to reach secular mind.

We need to know how the people we want to reach think.

PRACTICAL IDEAS

1. Observe for one month how the citizens around you behave, take notes and document without leaving comments: what is their philosophy of life, what they value, what they hate, etc.

2. Define if your community has a greater tendency to traditional secular or modern secular.

3. Make a list of topics from which you can reach your community socially.

4. Identify a viable service that your church can offer to your community.

5. Investigate how effective your church has been keeping the second and third generations of Adventists in recent years and make a plan to improve that picture.

Aim today by the grace of Christ, to reach someone you know with a postmodern mindset. God hates sin but loves the sinner; the blood of Christ also covers secular man.

SECTION II

The Urban Mission

This section seeks to revive the sense of mission of the remnant people; it outlines the distinctive features of the biblical prophets and draws an analogy between the prophetic mission of John the Baptist and the Seventh-day Adventist Church, there is also a dedicated space to analyze the implications of the third angel's message in the context of the evangelization of the cities

Chapter 3

The Mission of the Prophet

B Y MEDITATING ON the possible distinctive features of the biblical prophets, among other things, I rule out: gender, age, style, education, social class and profession. It is clear that God did not condition the prophetic call to any particular class or segment, Peter was a fisherman and Luke a physician, Solomon was a king and Amos a drover.[1] Paul and Timothy were used mightily by the Holy Spirit regardless of their age, the same way God enabled both men and women to transmit His will. Recall for example the prominent role of the prophetess Huldah in the time of King Josiah![2]

So, what is a prophet? What could be a common feature of all the prophets? Well! All were commissioned to communicate. The common denominator of the prophets is the message, not in their kind, such as: caution, warning or encouragement, but in the fact that all without exception, were called to proclaim a message.

Leon J. Wood says that:

"One of the reasons to explain the greatness of the prophets was their special call. They did not inherit this ministry; they were not born into a tribe or family of prophets. The fact of being a prophet's child did not give any promise of having the spirit of prophecy. Each prophet was individually selected by God and called to a specific task."[3]

It is true that for many a prophet is essentially someone who predicts the future, and actually Samuel predicted that the donkeys that had been lost to Saul's father had been found and Ahijah was blind but knew that the woman who came to visit in disguise was the wife of king Jeroboam and Elisha knew Gehazi received and hid money.

Even the Samaritan woman, excited by the revelation of his past said to Jesus: "Lord! I see that you are a prophet." But a careful study shows that the prophet is more than just revealing what is hidden.[4,5] *Navi,* of the most frequently used Hebrew words for prophet seems to have its roots in the idea of a messenger or one who proclaims a message.[6]

The scholar Abraham J. Hescher proposes:

> "It is the word of God when it descends on man which makes him a prophet.[7] Prophecy is God's voice to the silent agony. It is a way of living, a place where God and man meet each other."[8]

In fact, the prophet is not an echo, but the voice of God.

Consider following prophets, pay particular attention to the reason for the call that each received from the Lord:

God's reasons for the call	
Jonah	Get up and go to the great city of Nineveh, and deliver the message I have given you. (Jonah 3:2)
Jeremiah	"Alas, Sovereign Lord, "I said, "I do not know how to speak; I am too young." But the Lord said to me, "Do not say, 'I am too young.' You must go to everyone I send you to and say whatever I command you." (Jeremiah 1: 6,7)
Ezekiel	"Then He said to me: "Son of man, go to the house of Israel and speak with my words to them." (Ezekiel 3:4)
Paul	"Then Ananias answered, "Lord, I have heard from many about this man, how much harm he has done to your saints in Jerusalem. But the Lord said to him, 'Go, for he is a chosen vessel of mine to bear my name before Gentiles, kings, and the children of Israel." (Acts 9: 13- 15)

Phrases such as "... deliver the message I have given you", "... say whatever I command you", "...speak with My words to them" and "... go, for he is a chosen vessel of Mine to bear My name..." clearly establish that the message makes the prophet. What's more, the true prophet does not invent the message. He or she simply receives it and delivers it at the time and place indicated.

The prophet was called to communicate a divine message. The Seventh-day Adventist Bible Dictionary defines it as someone who first received God's instructions and then transmitted to people. The prophet speaks for God! Sticking to the task makes a prophet. The recipients of the message could change, the messenger style could be different, he was even allowed in many cases to choose his lexicon, but could not change the message. He could not, for example, conclude a war message as peaceful.

Prophet Amos affirms, "Surely the Lord God does nothing, unless He reveals His secret to His servants the prophets."[9]

A prophet is God's emissary, called to communicate His secrets. He is a messenger, but not in the sense of a simple carrier of news, the prophet is a friend and confidant. He can even argue with the Lord and ask him to change his will.[10]

The prophets were God's heralds (Ex. 7:1-2; Jer. 1:4-10). Their main role was to communicate God's words. As God's messengers they were not only to declare the truth. Their purpose was way beyond of just repeating what they heard. The prophets were preachers that communicated God's words in order to change their listener's way of thinking and behaving.[11]

The prophets are channels of divine mercy and even though they may be many, the message is essentially the same. This is the basic reason for the surprising connection of the Scriptures. This is the reason why a prophet of God who wrote about the year 70 AD, as did Judas, can freely express his message, proclaimed already by the prophet Enoch, the seventh since Adam.[12]

Tension between the prophets and the message

There is no prophet if there is no message! However throughout the Scriptures there is a certain tension between the messengers and the message "and" on more than one occasion, the Word became a source of anguish for the emissaries of God.

The prophet is a person, not a microphone. The prophet is someone that received a mission with the power of the word, that is not his or hers, and still has his or her own individuality. Sometimes the reaction to the divine message came by the influence of the same personality that presented the word. The prophet's mission is to communicate the divine vision, speaking God's word interpreted by his or her own situation.[13]

Jeremiah complained bitterly that the only messages he had were of destruction:

> Whenever I speak, I cry out proclaiming violence and destruction. So the word of the Lord has brought me insult and reproach all day long. But if I say, "I will not mention his word or speak anymore in his name," his word is in my heart like a fire, a fire shut up in my bones. I am weary of holding it in; indeed, I cannot."[14]

Beautiful! "I am weary of holding it in; indeed I cannot." The message is imposed upon the prophet, declining it is renouncing the prophetic call. Paul expressed it in the following:

> "For when I preach the gospel, I cannot boast, since I am compelled to preach. Woe to me if I do not preach the gospel!" [15]

An initial reaction to the prophetic order that deserves mention is that of Moses, a typical example of a prophet that at least at the beginning of his call, shrank to the message. Recall that when called he responded by saying: "What if they do not believe me or listen to me and say, 'The Lord did not appear to you'?" [16] The case of this Prophet reminds us that sometimes the weight of the message can overwhelm the prophet.

Thankfully, the Lord in his goodness encouraged the fearful messenger and proceeded to explain the plan, to which he replied, "Pardon your servant, Lord. I have never been eloquent, neither in the past nor since you have spoken to your servant. I am slow of speech and tongue."[17] Only to hear the solemn rebuke, "Who gave human beings their mouths? Who makes them deaf or mute? Who gives sight or makes them blind? Is it not I, the Lord? Now go; I will help you speak and will teach you what to say."[18]

The Lord's promise to his prophet is: I will be with your mouth. Although Moses argued against it, the call was irrevocable and God invoked His mandate. Such was the grace of God on this man that in his epitaph was written:

> "Since then, no prophet has risen in Israel like Moses, whom the Lord knew face to face, who did all those signs and wonders the Lord sent him to do in Egypt—to Pharaoh and to all his officials and to his whole land. For no one has ever shown the mighty power or performed the awesome deeds that Moses did in the sight of all Israel."[19]

The prophets are commissioned by God for great things, their words burn, their authority is that of the sender. The Scriptures tell how they faced kings, pharaohs and even entire villages. In the parable of the wicked tenants, the prophets are presented as collectors of God; their mission was to demand fruits worthy of repentance. [20] Extreme cases that catch the eye are those of Balaam, the "prophet" who bewitched by the gifts of foretelling, tried to change the message and Jesus the Prophet and God who died for not changing the message. [21]

Jerusalem in its impenitency became famous for mistreating and killing the prophets. In the second book of Chronicles it says:

> "The Lord, the God of their ancestors, sent word to them through his messengers again and again, because he had pity on his people and on his dwelling place. But they mocked God's messengers, despised his words and scoffed at his prophets until the wrath of the Lord was aroused against his people and there was no remedy."[22]

Going to Jerusalem was a kind of death sentence. Jesus described it as, "Jerusalem, Jerusalem, you who kill the prophets and stone those sent to you."[23] He went further, "how often I have longed to gather your children together, as a hen gathers her chicks under her wings, and you were not willing!"[24] God sent his prophets in order to gather His people under his wings, even the most fearsome messages were intended to redeem the people.

The church as a prophet of God

The church as a whole, besides personal responsibility, has been commissioned by God to deliver his message. In the apostolic commission Jesus emphasized:

> "Teaching them to observe all things whatsoever I have commanded you: and lo, I am with you always, even unto the end of the world. Amen." [25]

And the apostle Peter reminds us:

> "But you are a chosen people, a royal priesthood, a holy nation, God's special possession, that you may declare the praises of him who called you out of darkness into his wonderful light." [26]

People called to proclaim. This is a call to the prophetic ministry. Wouldn't you agree?

We have nothing to fear! Richard Bauckham, [27] discusses how God moves from just one to reaching the many, and reminds us of the example of Abraham, whom God called to bless all the families of the earth.[28] He also mentions Israel, the only nation to which God calls my own possession among all peoples, and then declares a kingdom of priests and a holy nation.[29] The theologian concludes with the statement of the Apostle Paul to the Corinthians:

> "... the foolish things of the world to shame the wise; God chose the weak things of the world to shame the strong. God chose the lowly things of this world and the despised things — and the things that are not — to nullify the things that are, so that no one may boast before him."[30]

Here God again make use of the 'less' to reach the most.

The secular mind has questions and expects answers from Christianity. Strong responses to its needs and miseries. The apostle Peter warns again:

> "... Always be prepared to give an answer to everyone who asks you to give the reason for the hope that you have."[31]

The gospel is good news and it is rightfully the church's responsibility to share it. It's the new voice crying in the wilderness! Whether by force of attraction or expansion as evangelistic strategies have differentiated centripetal and centrifugal of Israel and the early church respectively[32], the message has to be delivered.

People have the right to expect that church members may present their convictions in a persuasive and intelligent way. In fact, church members should be prepared to be challenged, truth is reasonable and has no fear to face opposition.[33]

Ellen G. White rightly said:

"From the beginning it has been God's plan that through His church shall be reflected to the world His fullness and His sufficiency. The members of the church, those whom He has called out of darkness into His marvelous light, are to show forth His glory. The church is the repository of the riches of the grace of Christ; and through the church will eventually be made manifest, even to "the principalities and powers in heavenly places" (Ephesians 3:10), the final and full display of the love of God."[34]

Michael Green offers five suggestions to Christian apologists, namely: start where the people you talk to are, this is to start where conversation flows, do not be embarrassed to open the bible, use it without authoritarianism, but authoritative; specialize in Jesus and resurrection, it is an unbeatable combination, distinguish between the smoke and the real problems, someone always wants to put one excuse after another, and finally be loving, but honest. After all, sooner or later everyone will have to face the question of Pilate: What to do with this Jesus called Christ?[35]

3rd Evangelistic Principle

Understand and accept our prophetic mission.

We have a message to deliver and it is urgent that we perceive the solemnity of the engagement. Time is running out and recipients await us!

PRACTICAL IDEAS

1. Name your favorite bible prophet and list the qualities you most admire in them.

2. Meditate on the corporate function of the church as God's prophet.

3. Write in a visible place two practical ways your congregation can fulfill their prophetic mission.

4. Define your roll in the prophetic mission of your local church.

Aim today by the grace of Christ to deliver the message that has been entrusted to you!

Chapter 4

A Prophetic People

MESSAGE THAT IS INSEPARABLE from the early church as prophetic community is proclaiming the kingdom of God,[1] to which the Scriptures refer to as present and future, all at once. When Jesus was asked by the Pharisees when the kingdom would come, he replied, "The coming of the kingdom of God is not something that can be observed, nor will people say, 'Here it is,' or 'There it is,' because the kingdom of God is in your midst."[2] But during his last supper, taking the cup: "... gave thanks and said, Take this, and divide it among yourselves: For I tell you I will not drink again from the fruit of the vine until the kingdom of God comes."[3]

Is the kingdom of God within us or no? Has it come or is it coming? Both. The Kingdom of God is now in the time of grace and soon it will be in glory. This explains the references to a throne of grace that we can come boldly to, as is emphasized in the letter to the Hebrews by declaring: "Let us therefore come boldly unto the throne of grace to receive mercy and find grace to help in time of need." And a throne of glory that will come into play at the time of the second coming, as reported by Matthew when he wrote: "When the Son of Man comes in his glory, and all the holy angels with him, then shall he sit upon the throne of glory."[4]

At this stage of glory only those whom God invite inherit the kingdom prepared from the foundation of the world. This distinction between these two great moments of the kingdom of God also explains why Jesus proclaimed in that particular context that his kingdom would not come with warning,[5] obviously referring to the stage of grace, as describing his coming in glory, compared with the lightning flashes and lights from one end of heaven to the other.[6]

Although the first advent materialized in a discreet and modest manger, the second coming, curtain of the kingdom of glory, will be with a shout, with the voice of the archangel and with the trumpet of God![7]

It is finished

You may wonder "Did not the kingdom of grace exist from Eden?" Ellen White clarifies the issue by saying:

> "The kingdom of grace was instituted immediately after the fall of man, when a plan was devised for the redemption of the guilty race. It then existed in the purpose and by the promise of God; and through faith, men could become its subjects. Yet it was not actually established until the death of Christ. ...When the Saviour yielded up his life and with his expiring breath cried out, "It is finished," then the fulfillment of the plan of redemption was assured. The promise of salvation made to the sinful pair in Eden was ratified. The kingdom of grace, which had before existed by the promise of God, was then established."[8]

I like to illustrate it by indicating that although the check was written in Eden, the deposit and payment was made on the cross. *It is finished*, is the hallmark of our debt cancellation. Glory to God!

The expression *it is finished* is mentioned by Jhon, on the occasion of the death of Jesus. We read:

> "When he had received the drink, Jesus said, 'It is finished.' With that, he bowed his head and gave up his spirit."[9]

That historical statement established the kingdom in its period of grace. Obviously a part of the plan of salvation was completed, the Lamb of God who takes away the sin of the world had been sacrificed, was now the priest, the same Christ in his role of mediator, a theme throughout the book of Hebrews.

It is importan to emphasize that the Greek verb here is *teleo*, which translates as finished, complete, execute, conclude, discharge a debt, pay, satisfy, terminate, finish, fulfill.

After his resurrection, Jesus spent forty days with his disciples speaking about the kingdom of God.[10] Over the next ten days between the ascension and Pentecost a beautiful party was celebrated in heaven because of His exaltation.[11] In his sermon at the Pentecost, the apostle Peter answers with powerful arguments to those who attributed drunkenness to the evident manifestation of the Holy Spirit:

We're not drunk, it is the fulfillment of the prophecy of the prophet Joel[12]

Jesus of Nazareth, whom you killed, is risen, destroying the pains of death, in fulfillment of the prophecy of King David about not letting your soul in hell or allowing your Holy One to see corruption.[13]

Resurrecting Jesus from the death was needed to fulfill the prophecy of offspring given to David, he was exalted by the right hand of God and received from the Father the promise of a Holy Spirit, the real consequence of what they saw and heard. [14]

The apostle Peter said in his sermon that day of Pentecost, was the beginning of the fulfillment of the prophecy of Psalm 110.[15]

1 The Lord said to my Lord: 'Sit at my right hand until I make your enemies a footstool for your feet.'

2 The Lord shall send the rod of thy Sion to Rule in the midst of your enemies.

3 Thy people shall be willing in the day of thy power, in the beauties of holiness. From the womb of the morning: thou hast the dew of thy youth.

4 The Lord has sworn and will not repent, Thou art a priest for ever after the order of Melchizedek.

5 The Lord at thy right hand shall strike through kings in the day of his wrath.

6 He shall judge among the nations, heaping up the dead; wound the heads over many countries.

7 drink of the brook in the way, so shall he lift his head.

Having seen the image from the Psalms let us now see the end of Peter's sermon:

32 This Jesus God raised up, whereof we all are witnesses.

33 Therefore being exalted to the right hand of God, and having received from the Father the promised Holy Spirit and has poured out what you now see and hear.

34 For David is not ascended into the heavens: but he saith himself, The Lord said unto my Lord, Sit at my right hand,

35 until I make thine enemies thy footstool.

36 Know therefore let all the house of Israel, that this Jesus whom you crucified, God has made him both Lord and Christ.[16]

Phrases such as, Sit at my right hand! You are a priest forever! God has made you Lord and Christ!, show that we must emphasize not only what happened on earth but what happened in heaven at Pentecost. Jesus, anointed as king and priest, began to minister with his own blood in the sanctuary! This leads us to the second 'It is finished', which closes the period of grace for God's kingdom and gives way to the period of glory.

Indeed a second *'It is finished'*[17] appears in the book of Revelation 16:17, during the last of the seven plagues that fall upon the earth. We know that the plagues begin to fall immediately after the end of the period of grace, note that in Revelation 15: 5-8, as the angels receive the bowls, the sanctuary was filled with smoke, symbol of a sanctuary where you cannot minister, which means without a mediator and without grace.[18]

Elena G. White states:

"Already a few drops of God's wrath have fallen upon the earth; but when the seven last plagues shall be poured out without mixture into the cup of His indignation, then it will be forever too late to repent and find shelter. No atoning blood will then wash away the stains of sin."[19]

And she also said that:

"It was impossible for the plagues to be poured out while Jesus officiated in the sanctuary; but as His work there is finished, and His intercession closes, there is nothing to stay the wrath of God, and it breaks with fury upon the shelterless head of the guilty sinner, who has slighted salvation and hated reproof. ... Then I saw Jesus lay off His priestly attire and clothe Himself with His most kingly robes. Upon His head were many crowns, a crown within a crown. Surrounded by the angelic host, He left heaven."[20]

With the second *'It is finished'* probation is closed and ends the second phase of the plan of salvation, Christ the priest, now takes mainly as King, beginning with his coming to the period of glory of his kingdom. The third 'It is finished' ends this tale of misery for good and sin and evil are destroyed forever, it is quite rightly stated in the context of the new heaven and the new earth of Revelation 21. It is written:

> "And he said, It is finished. I am the Alpha and the Omega, the beginning and the end. To the thirsty I will give from the spring of the water of life."[21]

The prophet Elijah and the kingdom of grace

The period of grace of God's kingdom was widely announced, when just before the first coming of Christ, John the Baptist came.[22] Matthew emphasizes:

> "In those days came John the Baptist preaching in the wilderness of Judea, saying, Repent, for the kingdom of heaven is at hand. For this is he that was spoken by the prophet Isaiah, saying, The voice of one crying in the wilderness: Prepare the way of the Lord, make his paths straight.[23]"

The way of the Lord should be paved, so established the Messianic prophecies.[24] Luke quotes Isaiah as follows:

> "Every valley shall be filled, and every mountain and hill made low. The crooked roads shall become straight, the rough ways smooth, and all flesh shall see the salvation of God."[25]

This powerful prophet named John, who would come in the power and spirit of Elijah, was also announced by the prophet Malachi.

> "Behold, I send My messenger, and he will prepare the way before Me. And the Lord, whom you seek, will suddenly come to His temple, even the Messenger of the covenant, in whom you delight. Behold, He is coming, says the Lord of hosts."[26]

Note that as in the prophecy of Isaiah the role of this messenger was to prepare the way for Jesus, The Lord or the Angel of the Covenant.

This coming to his temple alludes to Christ's ministry in the sanctuary, just what Jesus did after his death and resurrection. Concerning this, Ellen White says:

> "Christ had come, not to the earth, as they expected, but, as foreshadowed in the type, to the most holy place of the temple of God

in heaven. He is represented by the prophet Daniel as coming at this time to the Ancient of Days...[27] This coming is foretold also by the prophet Malachi... The coming of the Lord to His temple was sudden, unexpected, to His people. They were not looking for Him there. They expected Him to come to earth, "in flaming fire taking vengeance on them that know not God, and that obey not the gospel (2 Thessalonians 1:8)."[28]

Recall that John himself was questioned by the Pharisees if he was Elijah[29] to which he answered, I am the voice crying in the wilderness, alluding to the prophecy of Isaiah 40:3. However, Jesus openly called him the Elijah who was to come into the world.[30] It is not a reincarnation of the historical Elijah, but a prophet with similar qualities, and in fact the parallels between the two are amazing. John the Baptist connects the two dispensations; he was that lesser light which would be followed by a greater light.[31]

The prophet Elijah and the kingdom of glory

The prophet Malachi announces a second Elijah. In his fourth chapter, after mentioning the coming of the day as a fiery furnace in which some will be destroyed and others will rejoice, in a clear allusion to the contrast between the righteous and the wicked in the second coming, he states:

"Behold, I will send you Elijah the prophet before the coming of the great and dreadful day of the Lord. And he will turn the hearts of the fathers to the children, and the hearts of the children to their fathers, lest I come and strike the earth with a curse."[32]

This new prophet Elijah that Malachi announced is to prepare the way for the second coming, just as John prepared for the first advent, both the first and the second Elijah serve as the master of ceremony of the kingdom of God. To John was accounted the honor to declare "... Behold the Lamb of God who takes away the sin of the world."[33] The second Elijah shall declare:

"... Behold, this is our God, we have waited for Him, and He will save us. This is the Lord; we have waited for Him; we will be glad and rejoice in His salvation."[34]

But before he should fly across the sky with equal fervor proclaiming the third angel's message.

Ellen G. White explains:

Those preparing the way for the second coming of Jesus are represented by the faithful Elijah, as well as John came in the spirit of Elijah in order to prepare the way for the first coming of Christ.[35] "As a
prophet, John was 'to turn the hearts of the fathers to the children,
and the disobedient to the wisdom of the just; to make ready a people prepared for the Lord.' In preparing the way for Christ's first
advent, he was a representative of those who are to prepare a people
for our Lord's second coming."[36]

These statements clearly establish that John the Baptist, in
his eschatological application represents a prophetic people, who
are called to proclaim the second coming. Just as it was John's
responsibility to announce the first advent.[37] The two main characteristics of this people are:

- They keep the commandments of God and
- Posses the Spirit of Prophecy.[38]

It is a people of prophets! It is not in vain that it is ordered
of them: "You must prophesy again about many peoples, nations,
languages and kings."[39]

Morris L. Venden states in his book The Return of Elijah:

"The prophet hide himself for three and half years. We also noticed
that the prophecy of Daniel and Revelation another period of three
and half years, which is equivalent to 1,260 years. According to prophetic calculation, this period finished in 1798. If this is correct, then
the fulfillment of Elijah's coming would occur after 1798."[40]

The author also compares the essence of the message of
the three Elijah: The Tishbite,[41] John the Baptist and the third Elijah: The Seventh-day Adventist Church. The message of the first
clearly defines the path of the others

"And he answered, I have not troubled Israel, but thou and thy
father's house, have forsaken the commandments of the LORD and
followed the Baals."[42]

It is a call to return to God and his commandments![43]

The message that will stir the cities should be simple, but
powerful, like that of Elijah or Jonah, "Yet forty days, and Nin-
eveh shall be overthrown."[44] Jonah presented his message going
from one street to another. Then the message spread by word
of mouth, until everyone had heard the announcement.[45] It is
not necessary that we explain, in principle, all the details of the
Unknown God.[46] It will be enough to "not know anything among
you except Jesus Christ and Him crucified."[47]

It is noteworthy in this context how the name Seventh-day Adventists was selected. Regarding this, George R. Knight recounts that:

> "Many were inclined to the name Church of God, but the group did not accept because other denominations were already using it. Finally, David Hewitt suggested Seventh-day Adventists. This recommendation was accepted in order to express our faith and doctrine (RH, October 23, 1860, 179). According to the minutes of the session, Ellen G. White was silent, but after the fact she expressed her enthusiasm about the name. As an arrow will hit the transgressors of God's law, and call for repentance and faith in Jesus Christ."[48]

Obviously we can agree that the selection of our denominational name is no coincidence, but providence. Seventh-day Adventists, is the right name for the third Elijah![49] And in fact the essence of our message is in our name.

Pastor Ted Wilson in his book Almost Home, a call to revival and reformation, makes a solemn call to each Adventist to never forget their name. He further states that "like John we need to present a good example of our name in a pious lifestyle.[50] We are the people that bear the name of the Lord to proclaim the divine truth." [51] But where are we? Hiding in a cave or preaching at Carmel?

4th Evangelistic Principle

Mantain focus.

As Adventists we have to proclaim the kingdom of God, or give up the name. We are masters of ceremony of the glory of Christ's kingdom, as was John in the period of grace! Everything we do has to proclaim the glorious appearing of our great God and Savior Jesus Christ.[52]

PRACTICAL IDEAS

1. List the peculiar characteristics of prophet Elijah and contrast them to those of John the Baptist.

2. Compare the similarities between John the Baptist and the Seventh-Day Adventist Church.

3. Meditate on how leaders of Jesus' time even with the prophetic map in hand ignored the time of the coming of the Lord.

4. Reflect on how the name Seventh-day Adventists is closely related to our prophetic mission.

5. Share with your best friend ideas on how to strengthen the proclamation of the Second Advent.

Aim today by the grace of Christ to be active in proclaiming the second coming!

Chapter 5

Three Angels, One Gospel

THE LORD JESUS said in Matthew 24:14: "And this gospel of the kingdom will be preached in all the world as a witness unto all nations and then shall the end come." Revelation 14:6-20, gives details of the way in which this glorious prophecy will come to a happy fulfillment. The prophetic scenario is occupied by three angels flying in the midst of heaven having the everlasting gospel to preach unto them that dwell on the earth, to every nation, kindred, tongue and people[1], which then give way to the scene "... a white cloud, and upon the cloud one sat like unto the Son of man, having on his head a golden crown, and in his hand a sharp sickle."[2]

Who are these preaching angels flying through the midst of heaven? Why three? Are there three Gospels? Is it possible to identify any particular time for their prophetic ministry? What is the content? Ellen G. White solemnly wrote:

> "The most solemn, sacred work ever given to mortals is the proclamation of the first, second, and third angel's messages to our world."[3]

Preaching angels

An angel is a special messenger of God. In the Scriptures the expressions Mal'ak in Hebrew and angelos in Greek, both refer to supernatural beings, like humans, prophets and other persons that fulfilled this function.

God has assigned his messengers to specific functions at the discretion of His sovereign wisdom. This concept is clearly seen in the following texts:

> "So David sent messengers to Ishbosheth, Saul's son, saying, 'Give me my wife Michal, whom I betrothed to myself for a hundred fore-skins of the Philistines.' "[4]

> "Then Haggai, the Lord's messenger, spoke the Lord's message to the people, saying, 'I am with you, says the Lord.'"[5]

> "As they departed, Jesus began to say to the multitudes concerning John: 'What did you go out into the wilderness to see? A reed shaken by the wind?' "[6]

> "To the angel of the church of Ephesus write, 'These things says He who holds the seven stars in His right hand, who walks in the midst of the seven golden lampstands.' "[7]

Note that both David and John sent angels, that is messengers; the prophet Haggai came to town as an angel of God; the faithful witness instructed the apostle John to write to the angel of the church, that is the spiritual leader of the congregation to whom the letter was addressed, and concerning John, the Lord himself said, I send my messenger and he shall prepare the way, just as before coming a second time, the Lord sends his angels to prepare the way!

A second aspect to consider is that God assigned to the supernatural angels to be ministering spirits, sent forth to minister to those who shall be heirs of salvation.[8] That is the fundamental reason for their close cooperation with humans in proclaiming the good news of salvation. One case among many is recorded in Acts 8:26 - 38 when an angel of the Lord spoke to Philip and asked him to change the direction which he was going and evangelize an Ethiopian.

Both in Matthew 28: 18 -20 as in Acts 1:8 it is clear that God commissioned his human angels to preach the gospel. God in his infinite mercy placed the treasure in earthen vessels, that the excellency of the power may be of God and not from us.[9]

In his letter to the Corinthians the Apostle Paul reminds us that God has given us the ministry of reconciliation and uses phrases like:

> "...We are committed to use the word of reconciliation, we are ambas-

sadors for Christ, as if God is pleading through us: we implore you on Christ's behalf: Be reconciled to God."[10]

The three angels flying in the midst of heaven represent the remnant people of God in the fulfillment of his prophetic mission to proclaim the gospel to all nations as Christ prophesied in Matthew 24:14. This is the reason why the angels fly through the midst of heaven, and not the banks. It is a global mission!

Why three angels?

While there are three angels, there is only one gospel. Jesus called it the gospel of the kingdom. The apostle Paul: the gospel of God, the gospel of Christ, the gospel of the grace of God and the gospel of the glory of Christ[11] and John, the seer of Patmos, called it the everlasting gospel. These qualifiers are rather qualities of its own, distinctive and unique message.

Paul in his epistle to the Galatians warned that although some would pervert the gospel of Christ, they should not be believed and solemnly declared:

"But though we, or an angel from heaven, preach any other gospel to you than what we have preached, let him be accursed."[12]

The three angels represent three moments, three special emphasis on the revelation of this last message of warning to mankind, it is worth emphasizing that although the three angels flying together through the midst of heaven, do not come together at the sky, note the sequence:

1. I saw flying through the midst of heaven another angel, having the everlasting gospel to preach
2. And another angel followed, saying
3. And the third angel followed them, saying with a loud voice…[13]

The prophecies of Daniel 2, 7 and 8 with Revelation 13 and 14, signal the precise point at which these angels began and will end his ministry.

Clifford Goldstein in his book Graffiti in the Holy of Holies[14], summarizes the sequence of these three chapters of Daniel in the table below:

DANIEL 2	DANIEL 7	DANIEL 8
Babylon	Babylon	---
Medo-Persian	Medo-Persian	Medo-Persian
Greece	Greece	Greece
Pagan and Papal Rome	Pagan and Papal Rome	Pagan and Papal Rome
---	Judgement in Heaven	Cleansing of Sanctuary
SECOND COMING		

The point of Dr. Goldstein and many other exegetes is that these chapters are parallel[15], which means among other things, that the judgment in heaven and the cleansing of the sanctuary, both after pagan and papal Rome, are the same event.[16]

For his part, Dr. Jacques B. Doukhan in his book Secrets of Revelation emphasizes the parallels between Daniel 7 and Revelation 13 to 14, which in his opinion suggests that the message of the three angels in Daniel 7 corresponds to the time of judgment (Daniel 7:9-12), or Kippur (Daniel 8:14), which clarifies the following[17]:

Daniel 7	Revelation 13,14
Four beasts (lion, bear, leopard, beast with ten horns)	Beast with ten horns (characteristics of a lion, bear, leopard)
Oppressing Power (42 months)	Oppressing Power (42 months)
Judgement in Heaven	**Proclamation of the three angels**
Coming soon of man	Coming soon of man

This is very significant because when the first angel proclaims that the hour of judgment has come, he is referring to the judgment described by the prophet Daniel in chapter 7, which is equivalent to the cleansing of the sanctuary in Chapter 8. We know from the prophecies of Daniel 8:14 and Daniel 9:24-27, concerning the 2,300 days and 70 weeks respectively, the investigative judgment began on October 22, 1844.

Therefore, the message of the three angels extends from the great Millerite movement prior to 1844 until the second coming of Christ.[18]

The three angels preach the everlasting gospel to the entire globe; their route covers every nation, kindred, tongue and people. Their mission fulfills the preaching of the gospel to all ethnic groups (ethnos) and by extension to all population groups and sub groups, regardless of race, level of civilization, culture or socioeconomic status. Their mission includes from the largest cyber world called Facebook, to the smallest communities and the physically disabled. Dumb deaf communities, for example, are also waiting for the third angel! Their clear message implies:

- **Rejoice!** (Revere God, worship the Creator for the hour of his judgment is come)[19]
- **Proclamation!** (Babylon is fallen!)
- **Warning!** (If anyone worships the beast and his image and receives his mark and drink of the wine of the wrath of God).

Both the first and the third message are given in a loud voice.[20]

At first, the second angel did not proclaim his message in a loud voice, so it is repeated again by the mighty angel of Revelation 18, which joins the three angels and lightens the earth with his glory, cries out with a loud voice, Babylon is fallen! Ellen White expresses the power that this message proclaims in these two allusive quotations:

"The power which stirred the people so mightily in the 1844 movement will again be revealed. The third angel's message will go forth, not in whispered tones, but with a loud voice."[21]

"I saw that this message will close with power and strength far exceeding the midnight cry."[22]

The everlasting gospel and the prophet Elijah

Jesus proclaimed that He is the gospel when He read in Nazareth:

> "The Spirit of the Lord is upon me, because he has anointed me to preach good news to the poor, He has sent me to heal the broken-hearted, to preach deliverance to the captives and recovery of sight to the blind, to set at liberty those who are oppressed, to preach the acceptable year of the Lord."[23]

The prophet Isaiah foretold that the Messiah would come to evangelize (Isaiah 61: 1 -3). Christ took the scroll and read the prophecy, including the phrase "anointed Me to preach good news to the poor", evangelize in Greek evangelisastai, then proclaimed " ... Today this scripture is fulfilled in your hearing."[24] And it is that the everlasting gospel is proclaimed according to the Scriptures, as it was claimed by the apostles' preaching in Scripture.[25]

As Jesus read, He announced the year of goodness, but intentionally omitted the reference to the day of vengeance of our God[26] which is understandable, since that part of the prophecy was reserved for the end time. The everlasting gospel moves between grace and law, justice and mercy, between the years of kindness and the day of vengeance. Christ's command to his disciples and by extension to us is:

> "Teaching them to observe all things whatsoever I have commanded you: and lo, I am with you always, even unto the end of the world. Amen."[27]

The everlasting gospel is the same message of justification by faith. While in science $E=MC^2$, in theology Gospel = ministry of Christ as its best.

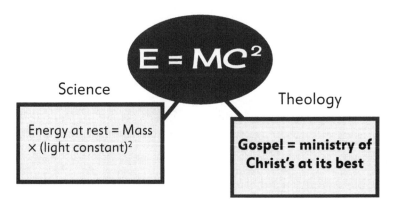

$$E = MC^2$$

Science

Energy at rest = Mass × (light constant)²

Theology

Gospel = ministry of Christ's at its best

Ellen G. White wrote in 1890:

"Several have written to me, inquiring if the message of justification by faith is the third angel's message, and I have answered, 'It is the third angel's message in verity.'"[28]

Finally, as noted, the relationship between the three angels and the third Elijah is directly proportional, because both groups represent the same people, The Seventh Day Adventist scholar Hans K. LA Rondelle expressed it in the following words:

"The Elijah message for the end time is developed by the Spirit of prophecy in Revelation 14: 6-12. Its worldwide proclamation will be continued by the second coming of Christ as King and Judge (cf. vv. -20 14), which defines the triple message as the call to wake up to prepare a people for the second coming of Christ."[29]

5th Evangelistic Principle

Keep the biblical route.

We are a people of preaching angels flying through the midst of heaven. We have to light the whole earth with the glory that comes from God.

PRACTICAL IDEAS

1. Read and meditate on the message of the three angels and their implications for cities.

2. Discuss with your family or study group the responsibilities of being angels of God.

3. Draw or ask a friend who has the gift to interpret the message of the three angels.

4. Identify a forgotten setting in your community and make an urgent plan to proclaim the three angels' messages.

5. Outline the relationship of the third angel with third Elijah.

Aim today by the grace of Christ, to include a place or population segment which is rarely visited in your missionary route.

SECTION III

The Enemies of Urban Evangelization

This section gives warning of the large internal enemies facing the church in fulfilling the gospel commission, namely apathy, complexes - evangelistic prejudices and discrimination, as well as biblical guidelines to address them.

Chapter 6

The Church in the Days of Noah

E KNOW FROM SCRIPTURE that we are facing a completely apathetic and secular world in these last days. It is written: "But as the days of Noah, so it will be the coming of the Son of Man. For as in the days before the flood they were eating and drinking, marrying and giving in marriage, until the day that Noah entered into the ark, And knew not until the flood came and took them all away, so also will the coming the Son of Man."[1]

They did not understand it until the flood came and carried them all. This is a generation that is not interested in the spiritual and yet needs to be reached. Their carelessness is such that its behavior is similar to that of the Sodomites. Regarding such Luke says:

> "Likewise as it was in the days of Lot: they ate, they drank, they bought, they sold, they planted, they builded; But the day Lot left Sodom, it rained from heaven fire and brimstone, and destroyed them all."[2]

It's sad but we are aware, the widespread disdain causes us to mourn but does not surprise us. What makes us concerned is not that the world is like the days of Noah, but that the church gets to be like Noah's contemporaries: Apathetic! Indifferent! Indolent! The lack of energy to face daily chores is the absolute indifference to everything. In general, apathy and discouragement are symptoms of depression.[3] Is the church living in a period of depression?

Jim George states that "apathy is equivalent to die by spiritual cold. If we expose ourselves to the extreme cold of ignorance compromise of principles, little by little we can experience the cold death of spiritual hypothermia."[4] We cannot deny apathy has clothed us for such a long time. Ellen G. White wrote, "The heathen in the cities at our doors have been strangely neglected."[5] In a second quote she comments:

> "It is a mystery that there are not hundreds at work where now there is but one. The heavenly universe is astonished at the apathy, the coldness, the listlessness of those who profess to be sons and daughters of God."[6]

To overcome apathy, behavior specialists recommend among other things:

- Acknowledge the state
- Find its source
- Deal with it responsibly and structure a new life plan to overcome the situation of inactivity.

Fortunately for the church the Holy Spirit is the antidote to apathy: a deadly poison of the old serpent. It is written:

> "But you will receive power when the Holy Spirit comes on you; and you will be my witnesses in Jerusalem, and in all Judea and Samaria, and to the ends of the earth."[7]

We can agree that a heart dynamited by the spirit has no room for laziness. Luke reaffirms by declaring. "When they had prayed, the place where they were assembled together was shaken, and they were all filled with the Holy Spirit and spoke boldly the word of God."[8] The response from the Spirit for apathy is boldness: courage, effort, audacity.

Listen or don't listen

The apostle Peter rightly called Noah a preacher of righteousness.[9] For a hundred and twenty long years he preached with a hammer as a microphone, as exposed by Ellen G. White: "Each hammer given in building the ark was a witness to the people," In a second comment on his long and faithful ministry, the prophetess points out:

"The message of Noah was to him a reality. Amid the scoffs and jeers of the world, he was an unbending witness for God. His meekness and righteousness were in bright contrast to the revolting crimes, intrigue, and violence continually practiced around him. A power attended his words; for it was the voice of God to man through His servant. Connection with God made him strong in the strength of infinite power, while for one hundred and twenty years his solemn warning voice fell upon the ears of the men of that generation..."[10]

Noah made a mark in his generation. No doubt about it.

The message must be proclaimed, whether the people listen or fail to listen. When God commissioned the prophet Ezekiel to speak on His behalf, he warned him that although he was not sent to a people of a hard language, but to his own people Israel, they would not want to listen because they had a hard front and stubborn heart. In this context God reveals himself to the Prophet and said:

"Behold I have made thy face strong against their faces, and thy forehead strong against their foreheads. As an adamant harder than flint have I made your forehead not, neither be afraid before them, they are a rebellious house."[11]

God told Ezekiel to not be afraid. Fear shuts down and stops the church. The disciples were paralyzed for fear after the crucifixion of Jesus, but once Jesus was raised from the dead, he appeared in their midst and said, "Peace be with you." Then he breathed on them the Holy Spirit.[12] And fear became courage. In front of a face of stone, stood a face of diamond. Perseverance, that's the secret.

The success of Noah was that he did not allow to be led by the mentality of those days. Noah was not deterred, he spoke and hammered! The church cannot afford to deviate from the mission and start living as in the days of Noah, our plans, resources, ministries, institutions ... must necessarily be focused on the mission, if we are not careful, the plague of indolence of the final days might infect us.

On April 16, 2012 ABC news surprised the world with the incredible story of Trish Vickers, a blind 59 year old English writer, who wrote 26 pages of her novel Grannifer legacy with a pen without ink. For two weeks, she worked thrilled and full of inspiration, in what would be her great work, but as she gave it to her son to read, became shocked with the sad reality that she had scribbled on paper, but the pen did not have any ink.[13] The mere fact of doing activities does not mean we are impacting or being relevant to our communities. This is also apathy!

If the church, the salt of the earth and light of the world really wants to glorify God it should take up the mission. Jesus said,

> "Ye are the salt of the earth: but if the salt has lost his savor, where-with shall it be salted? No good for nothing but to be thrown out and trampled by men."[14]

And after he encouraged his disciples to place their light on a stand, not under a bushel, he proclaimed,

> "Let your light shine before men, that they may see your good deeds and praise your Father in heaven."[15]

The apostle Paul reminds us that: God founded the church even "so that the manifold wisdom of God might now be made known through the church to the principalities and powers in the heavenly places."[16]

The Swiss theologian Emil Brunner, commenting on the missionary role of the church and its relation to the spiritual life, said: "The church exists for mission as fire exists for burning, when there is no mission there is no church and no faith."[17] Jesus established His church and ordained the twelve, so they would be with him and send them to preach: devotion and mission is the entirety of the Church.[18]

A dream worth telling

On September 29, 1886 Mrs. White had a dream in which she was picking strawberries in the city with a large entourage. Upon reaching the laden bushes she started collecting the nearby fruit carefully to avoid harvesting the green strawberries that were so mixed in with the ripe ones that you could only take one or two of each cluster, the others had already fallen to the ground and were half rotten. In astonishment she tells of the apathy of those who ate the provisions mindlessly, without remember-ing that their mission was to collect fruits. They complained that there were no strawberries in the low bushes, while still chatting, eating and complaining. Not to mention that even though there were plenty bags for work, they used it to hold their own food.

The author concludes:

"Thus the day wore on, and very little was accomplished. At last I said: "Brethren, you call this an unsuccessful expedition. If this is the way you work, I do not wonder at your lack of success. Your success or failure depends upon the way you take hold of the work. There are berries here; for I have found them. Some of you have been searching the low bushes in vain; others have found a few berries; but the high bushes have been passed by, simply because you did not expect to find fruit on them. You see that the fruit which I have gathered is large and ripe. In a little while other berries will ripen, and we can go over the bushes again. This is the way in which I was taught to gather fruit. ... You should be diligent, first to pick the berries nearest you, and then to search for those farther away; after that you can return and work nearby again, and thus you will be successful."[19]

A deaf bell

By analyzing some evangelistic aspects from the ten wise and foolish virgins, Ellen White refers:

"In the parable the wise virgins had oil in their vessels with their lamps. Their light burned with undimmed flame through the night of watching. It helped to swell the illumination for the bridegroom's honor. Shining out in the darkness, it helped to illuminate the way to the home of the bridegroom, to the marriage feast."[20]

It is not the same to sleep with lighted and oiled lamps than with lamps that are off and empty. Only those who keep their lamps filled with oil are true missionaries, the others will be overcome by spiritual indolence of the days of Noah. It was the encounter with Christ that converted the Samaritan woman into a missionary.

"Every true disciple is born into the kingdom of God as a missionary. He who drinks of the living water becomes a fountain of life. The receiver becomes a giver. The grace of Christ in the soul is like a spring in the desert, welling up to refresh all, and making those who are ready to perish eager to drink of the water of life."[21]

The church of the living God, cannot afford to compare itself with the proverbial Ambrosio's carbine.[22] Labriego of Sevillian origin, according to tradition, assaulted on roads with a rifle that was not loaded with gunpowder, but a type of bean, so the expression is applied to an useless object, something that does not fit where it was designed to fit. A kind of prophet with no message.

The largest bell in the world was cast in Russia in 1733 and weighs 216 tons, but unfortunately has never been rung because before it was installed it was stored in a warehouse that caught fire and to prevent the fire from melting it, they decided to throw water, which caused the overheated bell to crack. The world's largest bell never rang! A church without a mission, like a prophet without a message, is like a deaf bell.

The sixth principle is to accelerate the progress. God's response to the abundance of sin is over - abundance of grace, let us respond to worldly apathy with missionary fervor. Indifference against people for whom Christ died is an offense to God.

6th Evangelistic Principle

Accelerate the progress.

God's response to the abundance of sin is over - abundance of grace, let us respond to worldly apathy with missionary fervor. Indifference against people for whom Christ died is an offense to God.

PRACTICAL IDEAS

1. Reflect on the possible expressions of mission apathy of your local church and pray for them.

2. Identify your cracks and ask God to heal you and allow you to clatter with more intensity.

3. Suggest an area in your city where you would place a new strategic campaign.

4. Explain how you and your church are leaving a mark in your community.

Aim for the grace of Christ today to Dream! Hammer! Now!

Chapter 7

Giants in Canaan

WHY DID THE ISRAELITES who left Egypt refuse to possess Canaan? Sociologically the answer is simple: by prejudice! The sacred text reveals their thoughts by stating: "... The people who live there are powerful, and the cities are fortified and very large, and moreover we saw the children of Anak..." [1]

One could argue that the problem was their lack of faith and actually biblically these social attitudes are usually side effects of spiritual evil, yet psychosocial element analysis is equally significant. Consider the following statement:

> "But the men that went up with him said, We cannot attack those people, they are stronger than we ... The land we passed through to search it, is a land that devours its inhabitants, and all the people that we saw in midst of it are men of great stature. There we saw the giants, the sons of Anak, which come of the giants: and we were in our own sight as grasshoppers, and so we were in their sight."[2]

It's obvious that their main concern was the height of the inhabitants, especially the giant sons of Anak, whose exploits caused horror to them, creating the famous saying: Who can stand up against the Anakites?[3]

The theme of the giants in the Bible is recurrent, remember that Goliath measured up six cubits and a span[4], equivalent to about 9 feet (2.74 meters). King Og mentioned in Deuteronomy 3:11, slept on an iron bed nine cubits, about 14 feet (4.26 m.) long, reason which leads us to believe that he would have measured at least 12 feet (3.96 m.) tall.

Prejudice and evangelization

A prejudice is a preconceived attitude, lacking in evidence or adequate experience that tends to manifest in the form of sympathy or antipathy, against individuals, races, nationalities, institutions, patterns, ideas, experiences, etc. In our social structure the following types of prejudice are distinguished:

1. Social and economic prejudice,

2. Gender prejudice,

3. Ethnic and racial prejudice,

4. Religious prejudice,

5. Prejudice because of disability,

6. Prejudice because of image,

7. Prejudice because of age, among others. [5]

For Hans Georg Gadamer men are installed on prejudice, i.e., in a historical tradition into which they were born and developed and within which it is possible to dialogue and communication ... That is why Gadamer affirms that the prejudices of an individual are far more a reality in their life than reason or common sense.[6] The author also documents that precipitation is one of the main sources of prejudice. Any similarity to the case of Israel?

In general, two types of prejudices are distinguished: the positive and the negative. The former comes from a positive view of the object, although the object has not yet been investigated, while in the second case a negative view of the object is held also without knowing the reality of the object. The positive bias predisposes an approach, while the negative bias leads to intellectual resistance, resulting in a certain mental barrier that antagonizes one as they approach the object.[7]

A famous fatal prejudice among some Christian communities is that 'the rich are not interested in the gospel', that is the tendency to think that if the house is luxurious, its inhabitants are materialistic. These prejudices obviously segregate evangelism, but is the church really benefitted by the 'positive' prejudices or do they produce evangelistic biases?

Prejudices are based mainly on stereotypes and categorizations, while evaluative beliefs, be they positive or negative, are accepted as criteria of truth. It is a form of labeling the world, amongst other things, in the light of our experiences, beliefs and needs; this way we are distorting and limiting our social relations.

Racial stereotypes are common in sports. Perry and Darley in 1997 confirmed that Americans believe that whites don't know how to jump. According to this stereotype black basketball players are by nature superior in athletic skills. In contrast to white players, they are erroneously perceived as more intelligent and dedicated. The same phenomenon occurs in politics, religion, evangelism and other social contexts. [8]

Humans tend to catalog the world. We tend to classify everything that exists to know it better, so we talk about tall and short, beautiful and ugly, but stereotypes go beyond because they include personality traits, emotions, hobbies, tastes and spiritual aspects ... that is thought to be shared by members of a group, violating in many cases the biblical principle of not judging lest we be judged.[9]

Indeed Dennis Coon defines stereotypes as "oversimplified images of the members of a group."[10] If one is tall, good-looking and travels in a luxury vehicle, do not waste your time preaching to him. Muslim equals danger. The black are tough. These are rude examples of racial prejudice. How sad!

The truth is that prejudices are rooted in our ideologies and lifestyles and are difficult to change.

Now why consider an issue like this in the context of evangelization? Because especially in religious matters, prejudices are highly exclusive; they produce evangelistic paralysis, hence the importance of knowing them, knowing how they arise, how to avoid them and how to remove them from our staff and church environment.

We seemed like grasshoppers. A complex?

It's one thing to be prejudiced and a different, but equally damaging thing is to be subject of prejudice. John the Baptist suffered the affront of many of his contemporaries, who considered him to be a simple reed moved by the wind, when in fact he was more than a prophet. [11]

In the expression: "... and we were in our own sight as grasshoppers, and so we seemed to them"[12] we can evidence the feeling of superiority of these Canaanites and discrimination towards God's people, but we can also observe complexes in some of the princes of Israel themselves.

A complex is a feeling, generally of inferiority, producing a shy or inhibited behavior, and the stigmas in those that are objects, sometimes collectively, that can be generated are dangerous personal disorders, especially in sensitive subjects.

Complexes largely stem from comparisons and are strongly related to self-esteem. The big problem with complexes is that they own and imprison us. "Complexes interfere with the intention of will and alter the activity of consciousness."[13]

There is, moreover the danger of believing ourselves to be giants and generators of prejudices and complexes. Christ our example, never did this, instead he ate with publicans and sinners.[14] Ellen G. White warned:

> "Today the truth is to be proclaimed to all nations and kindreds and tongues and peoples. Christ desires us to labor in a way that will not arouse prejudice, for when prejudice is aroused, some are cut off from hearing the truth..."[15]

Always remember that the Giants do not survive and that Christ broke down the dividing wall.[16]

How to overcome prejudice?

How many Adventists are ridiculed by expressing their agreement with a literal and recent creation? How many are accused of not eating, bathing or even brushing on Sabbath? Our brothers and sisters must be taught how to handle these prejudices. A good way to shield against them is becoming aware of the God whom we serve and of the call we have answered.

The apostle Paul was emphatic :

> "I am not ashamed of the gospel, for it is the power of God for salvation to everyone who believes, first to the Jew first and also to the Greek."[17]

His preaching focused on Christ crucified, a stumbling block to Jews and foolishness to Gentiles, but to the apostle, power and wisdom of God.[18]

Sociologists argue that prejudice can be reduced as contacts narrow down and perception of reality becomes more accurate; prejudices tend to move away, but in order to overcome them we must educate ourselves on the subject of prejudice. When Nathanael asked the prejudiced question if anything good could come out of Nazareth, Philip only replied, "come and see."[19] One meeting was enough.

As Nathanael physically approached Jesus, He expected him empathetically. An effective way to change attitudes is to develop empathy, to put ourselves in the place of others. It is expected that members of different groups working to eliminate their prejudices have the same status and pursue joint activities, always in cooperation and never in competition.

Daniel and his friends knew in whom they had believed, so that when they were faced with prejudice against the effectiveness of a vegetarian diet, spoke directly about their beliefs and principles:

> "Please test your servants for ten days, and let them give us vegetables to eat and water to drink. Then let our appearance be examined before you, and the appearance of the young men who eat the portion of the king's delicacies; and as you see fit, so deal with your servants."[20]

Despite Einstein's famous saying that it is easier to disintegrate an atom than a prejudice, you can confront prejudice like this: try me, know me and you will see. If your neighbor thinks you do not eat on saturdays, a simple invitation to lunch is good enough, it's amazing the doors that a gesture of courtesy can open.

> "From prejudice reasoning is not released one, as is commonly believed naively. Nothing to argue before the beliefs, the unique opportunity to oppose them is judicious destroy evidence."[21]

Modern giants

The XXI century church is challenged to possess Canaan. It's hard to imagine a generation that welcomes the next century, and what about our prejudices? Residential quarters declared impenetrable! Secularism made of steel! High towers which we are locusts compared to them! Our prejudices can become our main evangelistic barrier or we can decide to move forward by faith and crush the obstacles.

Israel's response was mournful; as a modern Israel we have to respond differently. It is written: "So all the congregation lifted up their voices and cried, and the people wept that night."[22] On this sad scene Ellen White comments :

> "As the people listened to this report they gave vent to their disappointment with bitter reproaches and wailing. They did not wait and reflect and reason that God, who had brought them out thus far, would certainly give them the land. But they yielded to discouragement at once. They limited the power of the Holy One and trusted not in God, who had hitherto led them."[23]

Although Caleb and Joshua encouraged the people arguing that they would eat them like bread,[24] the people did not listen but talked about stoning them. Forty years later, Caleb son of Jephunneh according to the commandment of the LORD to Joshua, received the city of Arba the father of Anak. "And Caleb drove out the three sons of Anak: Sheshai, Ahiman, and Talmai, the children of Anak."[25] The sons of Anak were real, but the God of Israel, whose glorious manifestations had been so obvious was too and still is real.

The best way to face our fears and banish prejudices and complexes, is faith in the God of our history.

The Book of the Apostles chapter 10 is a good example of how God finally dodged the barrier of prejudice to advance the gospel in the early church:

> "God's role is to destroy the giants. The part is played by his people trust him to do that and keep your eyes on the one for whom there are no giants."[26]

Caleb and Joshua remained free of complexes and prejudices because they knew in whom they had believed. Today the formula remains exactly the same. Ellen G. White confirmed this idea when she wrote:

> "We have nothing to fear for the future, except as we shall forget the way the Lord has led us, and His teaching in our past history."[27]

7th Evangelistic Principle

Crush prejudice.

We have to keep conquering giants, although modern cities are planted with tall towers and overwhelming structures, our God is great and powerful. We are not ashamed of the gospel because it is the power of God!

PRACTICAL IDEAS

1. Evaluate your personal prejudices and decide to face them in the name of the Lord.

2. Reflect on your own complexes and seek help to overcome them.

3. Challenge your small group or church to conquer Canaan for Christ.

4. Make a list and your giant presents God with faith and prayer.

5. Encourage your church to remove barriers that negatively project in your community.

Aim today by the grace of Christ, to overcome your fears, prejudices and complexes, and conquer your neighborhood, school or work colleagues for the kingdom of God!

Chapter 8

Modern Samaritans

J ESUS CLEARLY TRACED the missionary path for his disciples by declaring : "... You will be my witnesses in Jerusalem, throughout Judea, in Samaria, and unto the uttermost part of the earth."[1] While every aspect of the commission was challenging, the test remained reaching the Gentiles, beginning with the Samaritans, who were systematically overlooked.

This discriminatory attitude can be seen during the persecution after Stephen's death. Luke narrated:

> "At that time a great persecution arose against the church which was at Jerusalem; and they were all scattered throughout the regions of Judea and Samaria, except the apostles."[2]

Samaria? Would this ceaseless hunt be converted into a unique opportunity to complete the task? It should be recalled that this incident took place in 34 AD, three and a half years after the death of the Messiah, which means that the seventy weeks determined upon the Jewish nation had just finished.[3] It was time to impact the Gentiles with the gospel, but were Christians ready for such a challenge?

Some, yes! Philip went down to Samaria and preached Christ, whom they had met in person, after his conversation with the Samaritan woman. Jesus was strongly interested in the evangelization of the Samaritans, passing through Samaria and then sending of the seventy confirms this.[4]

Regarding this Ellen White said :

"The Saviour's own visit to Samaria, and later, the commendation of the good Samaritan, and the grateful joy of that leper, a Samaritan, who alone of the ten returned to give thanks to Christ, were full of significance to the disciples. The lesson sank deep into their hearts. … When in their Master's name they went to Samaria…. After His ascension they welcomed the Saviour's messengers, and the disciples gathered a precious harvest from among those who had once been their bitterest enemies."[5]

The answer to Philip's preaching was particularly blunt! The testimony of Scripture is that there was great joy in that city.[6] However, even among many fellow Jews, everything to the Gentiles was highly suspicious. Peter himself was interrogated for the crime of preaching and baptizing in the house of Cornelius.[7]

After an interlude to discuss the evangelization of Ethiopia, Saul's conversion and repentance of Cornelius, essentially related to the Gentiles preaching texts, Luke resumes his account of the flight commenting:

"Now those who were scattered because of the persecution that arose because of Stephen traveled as far as Phoenicia, Cyprus and Antioch, speaking the word to no one but unto the Jews only."[8]

The great omission

Why only the Jews? Didn't Jesus say: Jerusalem, Judea, Samaria and to the ends of the earth? It's the sad old story, the same as Jonah's! Charting our own path, affected by our own prejudices. These good brothers and sisters were willing to die for their faith, left father, mother, possessions, but excluded from their preaching those who were not Jews. They were missionaries! But selective.

It is a fact, prejudice will lead to discrimination! The gospel must go to the ends of the earth; the last corner, the last race, the last layer … there is no room for derangement. Everyone has the right to hear the word and decide whether they believe it.

A selective obedience to the gospel requirements is to some extent a Christianized version of Jewish ethnocentrism of the first century. This emotional tendency of the culture makes the sole discretion to interpret the behavior of other groups, races or societies.[9] And typically involves the belief that one's own ethnic group's cultural, religious, linguistic or socially important or superior to those of other cultures.[10]

Seventh-day Adventists in particular, we must remember that Christ is the light that illuminates the entire world.[11] And as Paul specifically told the Corinthians, we know in part and we prophesy in part, by looking through a dark glass.[12] The religious ethnocentrism is not well seen by postmodernists and by heaven either, it is better to be humble!

Dimensions of the mission

For teaching purposes I like to imagine God's mission entrusted to the church in two dimensions: a prophetic and an apostolic. The prophet delivers a message, whether they listen or not, and the church is committed to deliver its message in the same conditions. If it is well received, it is the duty of the apostle to continue the missionary work so listeners become disciples of Christ, if not received, there will come a time that he will shake the dust off his shoes.[13] Although the mission seeks to make disciples, it begins by announcing the gospel by precept and example.

I think the following statement by Ellen White goes in these terms:

> "The church is God's appointed agency for the salvation of men. It was organized for service, and its mission is to carry the gospel to the world."[14]

Paul emphatically asks :

> How, then shall they call on Him in whom they have not believed? And how shall they believe in him of whom they have not heard? And how shall they hear without a preacher?[15]

The church does not end when it proclaims the Gospel, it is just beginning! It is our duty to notify the gospel to all, and disciple those who believe. Our mission embraces all humanity, not just the tiny group who decides to believe.

> "The world's Redeemer had many hearers, but few followers. Noah preached one hundred and twenty years to the people before the Flood, and yet there were few who appreciated this precious, probationary time. Save Noah and his family, not one was numbered with the believers and entered into the ark. Of all the inhabitants of the earth, only eight souls received the message; but that message

condemned the world… Our message to the world will be a savor
of life unto life to all who accept it, and of condemnation to all who
reject it."[16]

Bold!

Luke, a gentile, warns excitedly as he continues his story:

"But some of them were men of Cyprus and Cyrene, who, when
they came to Antioch, spoke unto the Grecians, preaching the Lord
Jesus. And the hand of the Lord was with them: and a great number
believed and turned to the Lord."[17]

Barnabas and Paul continued the beautiful work of discipleship for a year, a great many people were added, and the disciples were called Christians first in Antioch.[18] What great lesson
for us? The great truth is that the church stopped growing when
it stopped talking and began to grow again when it continued to
spoke.

To McGavran, a third-generation missionary who served
35 years in India, growth is the sine qua non of the mission, i.e.
if the mission is fulfilled there has to be growth.[19] "As soon as
a church implements a strategy to reach people, growth can be
expected."[20]

Paul inspires us with his example by stating:

" … first unto them of Damascus, and at Jerusalem, and throughout
all the land of Judea, and to the Gentiles, that they should repent and
turn to God, performing deeds repentance. For these causes the Jews
caught me in the temple, tried to kill me. Having therefore obtained
help of God, I continue unto this day, witnessing both to small and
great, saying none of the things which the prophets and Moses said
would happen. "[21]

Shocking! Paul began to testify in the same place where
Christ met him, he did not discriminate between Jews and Gentiles, but preached to large and small, kings and slaves. So it is
written. Interestingly, in the Scriptures there is no gift of witnessing, although there is of evangelist.[22] "A witness is someone who
can attest to something."[23] And we all have been called to testify
to all about Jesus.

Sadly most of us have our own Samaria, our local gentiles. Those are the social, ethnic, cultural, intellectual, economic

or religious differences, those who are intentionally overlooked, and whom we have had the luxury of deciding, claiming they would not believe. The rich, disabled, addicts, beggars, members of other religious congregations, political, minority groups are just some of those cases that could be among our favorite Gentiles.

There is the danger of isolating ourselves rather than separating from the world.

Jesus prayed:

> " My prayer is not that you take them out of the world but that you protect them from evil. They do not belong to the world, as I am not of the world. Sanctify them through thy truth: thy word is truth As you sent me into the world, I also sent them into the world. "[24]

Luis Sáez, a discipleship expert says:

> "We need love, strength and discernment to know what we share with non-believers and how to communicate in a loving way that we cannot participate with them in certain things. The problem with many of us is that after being in the church for some time have increasingly less incredulous friends."[25]

Phillip G. Samaan challenges us to remember that it is the salt which takes the initiative: penetrating, invading. "It spreads through food (not vice versa)."[26]

Get to work!

In his article, "The Great Omission" Dr. Gregg Detwiler, director of Intercultural Ministries of the Emmanuel Gospel Center, says this great danger of exclusions in fulfilling the mission and invites the church of God to overcome utilizing Jesus' model, as is clear from his encounter with the Samaritan woman. He says that if we are really determined to reach our nations, we should ponder the following:

- **Be intentional.** For Christ to cross Samaria, it was much more than a geographical duty, it was a spiritual duty, (thousands of Jewish travelers preferred to go around the Jordan Valley, submitting themselves to a painful and dangerous journey.)

- **Crossing barriers.** Christ crossed at least four: a geographical barrier, a cultural, a gender and finally the barrier of sin.

- **Use spiritual resources.** Christ offered living water.

- **Wait for transformations.** Not only the woman was transformed, but those who lived around her were also transformed. As we work with our gentiles, we can expect many surprises.

"Jesus had to go through Samaria because it was not in his way, but because it was in his mind. It was on purpose and not by accident. In fact, as the text says, it was necessary, but the need was in Him and not in the circumstances."[27]

Go thou and do likewise!

8th Evangelistic Principle

Focus on those overlooked.

God has ordained us to carry the gospel also to Samaria. "He is no respecter of persons: But in every nation the man that fears him and works righteousness."[28]

PRACTICAL IDEAS

1. Make a list of people you have overlooked in your community.

2. Identify your groups of modern day Samaritans.

3. Make a plan to visit your favorite Samaritans.

4. Create the good habit of inviting someone in need to eat.

5. Pass by your Samaria and ask for a drink.

6. Identify possible 'gentiles' at your workplace.

7. Practice new forms of teaching the truth with humbleness.

8. List minority groups, foreigners, seniors of your community.

9. Identify and visit some neighbor whom you fear or whom you have never preached the Word of God to.

Aim today by the grace of Christ to preach the gospel to all you can without discrimination!

The Challenges of Urban Evangelization

This section discusses the need for scientific and technological tools available in building the kingdom of God, which among other things includes some ideas on how to raise relevant information to the community and integrate them into a local strategic plan in order to potentialize practical evangelistic work. It also studies the role of the media in evangelism and the ministry of small groups and other evangelistic methods, of no lesser importance. It also considers the urgency to strengthen the role of youth and children in the advancement of the ever-lasting gospel, and well-defined structure plans to achieve the average, high and special class groups.

Chapter 9

Running with the Horsemen

THE INGENIOUS HIDALGO DON QUIXOTE fought against windmills, but not us, indeed, we don't even fight against flesh and blood, but against the rulers of darkness and spiritual wickedness in high places.[1] Therefore, we must march in order! That Jehovah will fight for us is no excuse for the lack of organization. There is no contradiction between "The Lord will fight for you. Rest assured"[2] and the following verse: "... Why are you crying out to me? Tell the Israelites to go forward."[3] The first is an invitation to trust, not to wander and the second is a call to do our part.

The story of Gideon reveals how he divided his three hundred men into three companies to create the illusion that the enemies were surrounded by a large army, and his ingenious tactics to start blowing trumpets at midnight, just as they had the sentinels, i.e. at a strategic time.[4]

Ellen White explains:

"By divine direction a plan of attack was suggested to him, which he immediately set out to execute. The three hundred men were divided into three companies. To every man were given a trumpet, and a torch concealed in an earthen pitcher... In every direction was heard the sound of trumpets, with the cry of the assailants. Believing themselves at the mercy of an overwhelming force, the Midianites were panic-stricken. With wild cries of alarm they fled for life, and, mistaking their own companions for enemies, they slew one another."[5]

It is also inspiring to see how God integrates planning and spiritual preparation. Gideon had to declare war on the idolatry of his father before God could use him.[6] Joshua had to circumcise the Israelites again and celebrate the Passover with the people before driving his draft surround Jericho for seven days.[7] And Moses was severely rebuked by the Lord because of their indolence to circumcise his son Eliezer, while returning to Egypt with the plan to liberate the Jews.[8,9]

Revival and a new paradigm

God has arranged for revival and reformation to walk hand in hand. While revival is a spiritual resurrection, reform is a new way of doing things. It's a paradigm shift!

In 1902 Ellen White emphasized:

"A revival and reformation under the ministration of the Holy Spirit must be made. Revival and reformation are two different things. Revival signifies a renewal of spiritual life, a quickening of the powers of mind and heart, a resurrection from spiritual death. Reformation signifies a reorganization, a change in ideas and theories, habits and practices. The reform will not bring forth the good fruit of righteousness unless it is connected with the revival of the spirit. Revival and reformation are to do the appointed work, and in doing this work both should be combined."[10]

A change in ideas and theories, habits and practices is a paradigm shift. That's it! If at any time the church needed reform it is now and this implies openness to new ways of doing things.

The writer and prophet, Ellen G. White also stressed :

"Men are needed who pray to God for wisdom, and who, under the guidance of God, can put new life into the old methods of labor and can invent new plans and new methods of awakening the interest of church members and reaching the men and women of the world."[11]

It is dangerous to close the mind by the simple fact that it is new. It has been said that the mind is like a parachute and it only works when opened. The Swiss seriously depleted its leadership in the watch market for being slow to accept the quartz watch, from 65 % control of the market in 1968 to less than 10 % when Japan came out with the new paradigm they had discarded. We know the phrase, "Not even the best watchmakers can stop the time."[12]

Coca - cola lost millions of dollars when, on April 23, 1985, it decided to change its formula and to launch the new Coca - cola (New Coke), in what is considered one of the worst marketing mistakes of history; consumers rebelled and the original formula had to return to the market as Coca Cola Classic (Coke Classic).

On the contrary, the world's most recognizable commercial icon, the Contour Bottle by Coca -Cola itself, since 1916 has had all sorts of versions, sizes and materials, including the El Salvador plastic bag or bottle made from plants distributed in Denmark, the company reinventing and making millions of dollars.

As a church we should not negotiate the biblical foundations of our faith, but we can evaluate our presentation and make it more friendly and empathetic as well as designing new ways to conquer cities and retain people.

A spiritual business

At this point I wonder, is it possible to achieve cities without specific well articulated plans? Of course not! What is our strategy for reaching the deaf? The blind? The rich? Ellen G. White states :

"All Heaven is in activity, and the angels of God are waiting to cooperate with all who will devise plans whereby souls for whom Christ died may hear the glad tidings of salvation."[13]

Clearly danger does not lie in planning but when our plans do not harmonize with the plans of God.

The church is a spiritual enterprise that runs at this track called world against the thousands of sin providers; promoters of entertainment, of pornography and greed. It's an age-old struggle that gets stronger every day. I wonder : How well do we run? Are we behind or ahead of our competitors?

It is in our interest to reflect upon this in light of the Scriptures:

"If thou hast run with the footmen, and they have wearied you, how canst thou contend with horses? ..."[14]

Worldly companies are organized every day, are equipped technologically, innovate and invest often in human development of its staff. We have to realize that the world has changed and act accordingly. We do not fight against windmills. Therefore we should not fight like one who is striking the air.

What company today would give into the luxury of advancing without a clear definition of mission, vision and values? Or without a strategic plan? What organization would dare plan without investigating? Who would enter in a new market without a strategy to position your brand? We run with the horsemen. We need to use science!

Whether we want to or not, we are running alongside a world of the twenty-first century, but with a XXII century mentality, not the world of IXX century. It is our challenge to run well for the glory of God and the blessing of His cause.

Urban tools

It is very important to know the social purposes of planning evangelistic events, since an urban mind implies an urban strategy and to plan for the secular mind demands knowledge of the secular mind. This is where disciplines such as sociology, applied statistics and social research can enhance evangelization.

The prominent sociologist of Andrews University, Lionel Matthews said:

"Sociology is a useful tool for Christians, since... through it you can get the much needed understanding of the social world."[15]

Urban sociology, in turn, studies human interaction in metropolitan areas and integrates quantitative and qualitative research methods to propose improvements in levels of living. These twinned with theology and science in the service of the Great Commission could be of great blessing to build the kingdom of God. It possibly calls for reengineering our missionary and evangelistic strategies!

Only in the area of qualitative research do we have the help in the following possibilities:

- Phenomenological studies (They deal with the experience)
- Grounded theory studies (build significant theories subjects studied)

- Case studies (deeply explore a contemporary phenomenon in its real context of existence.)
- Research - action (studies are performed on the practice)
- Ethnographic studies (They deal with the culture)

On the *ethnographic method*, Vieytes Ruth explains:

"Their goal is to provide a way of understanding culture as a whole that encompasses beliefs, customs, knowledge and standards, capabilities and habits acquired by man - and to be a member of society."[16]

This could be a very useful tool for our missionaries in foreign and local lands! Whenever possible, we must know as much as possible about the people we intend to evangelize.

Quantitative techniques use surveys, sampling or census as basic raw material. The basics here include instrument validity, selection and sample size and relevance of the statistical treatment given to the data. Sampling techniques should be noted rigorously, confidence levels should be respected and margins of error minimally accepted.

The need of questions

The church must ask questions and seek answers. It was a question that prompted Donald A. McGavran to get started in the interesting field of social research applied to church growth. He wanted to know: How do people become Christian? His response led him to become the father of church growth.

Christ Himself said to Peter, Whom do men say that the Son of Man is?

Sociologists say that perception is as important as reality itself, how people perceive us? What do men say is the Adventist Church ? We could be surprised by the answers!

"And they said, Some say John the Baptist, others Elijah, still others Jeremiah or one of the prophets. He said unto them, But who do you say that I am? Simon Peter answered and said, You are the Christ, the Son of the living God. Jesus replied, Blessed are you, Simon son of Jonah, for flesh and blood has not revealed this to you, but my Father who is in heaven."

What do our friends say? What do our members say? And above all, what does God say ? Interesting questions!

In 2004 an Adventist Conference in the Dominican Republic asked itself questions and decided to consult 8,790 families living around its more than two hundred congregations.[17] The author had the honor of leading this investigation. What follows are some questions and answers :

1. Are you actively attending any church?

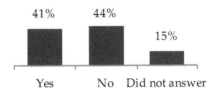

41%	44%	
Yes	No	Did not answer
		15%

2. If yes, please indicate which one?

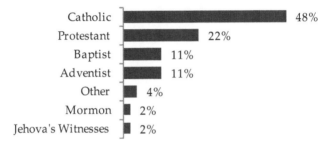

Catholic — 48%
Protestant — 22%
Baptist — 11%
Adventist — 11%
Other — 4%
Mormon — 2%
Jehova's Witnesses — 2%

3. Why do you think that many people do not attend church?

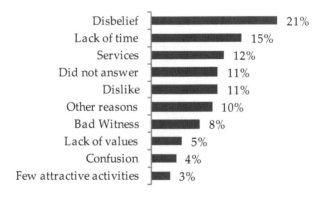

Disbelief — 21%
Lack of time — 15%
Services — 12%
Did not answer — 11%
Dislike — 11%
Other reasons — 10%
Bad Witness — 8%
Lack of values — 5%
Confusion — 4%
Few attractive activities — 3%

4. If you were to seek a church to attend what do you expect it to have?

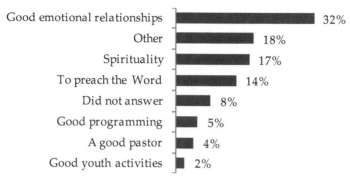

These responses alone should be enough to shake the foundations of our evangelistic vision.

5. What advice would you give to a pastor who really wants to help people?

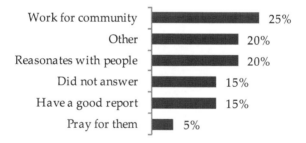

6. Is there anything I can do for you?

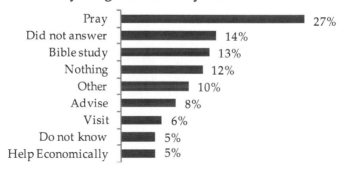

7. What does the name Seventh-day Adventist mean to you?

This question is fundamental because it reveals the positioning of our name (brand) in the market.

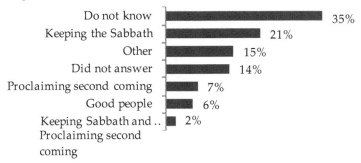

Remember we questioned neighbors of our churches, some of which had been there for years.

8. If you came to visit our church, Saturday morning which of these times would be better?

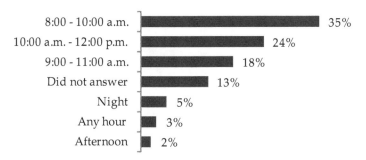

It is obvious that many people prefer a schedule that allows them to worship and then continue with their chores. I like the idea, Faith comes by hearing![18]

As you can observe, these responses are a real mine. Companies use data mining as a useful tool in their strategic planning. Research is not an end in itself, it's a gift from God and should be at the service of the Great Commission, this philosophy is what has given success to the work of Christian Schwarz and the tenets of 'Natural Development churches.'

The church and research

Some years ago the General Conference of Seventh-day Adventists established at Andrews University the Global Research Center which supports the strategists and monitor the health and growth of the church worldwide. This initiative should be replicated in each division and if possible in each country.

Under the subtitle, Research and the future of the Seventh-day Adventist Church, Erich W. Baumgartner, who precisely works in the Global Research Center at Andrews, expressed the following considerations:

- Modern organizations cannot function effectively without adequate information.

- Research provides the information necessary to develop, monitor, evaluate and improve the missionary strategies.

- Research is an important leadership role in modern organizations operating the mission in the information era.

- Research provides useful information for decision-making. However, researchers need to know how to pour it into strategic decisions.

- Leaders, who are constantly confronted with the needs of the moment, need help and specific training in the strategic use of information.

The birth of a business

Every moderately organized company will have a declaration of its mission statement, vision, values and logo, along with a balanced strategic planning and institutional manual for guidance. These operational issues along with the legal aspects, are the birth of the company. The Seventh-day Adventist Church has its birth certificate.

Sadly, however, many of these elements fail to land at our church organizations much less to local congregations. If you decide at this time to investigate, you will realize that every day a greater number of establishments have hung their mission statement, vision and values in a conspicuous place; although we have made progress, our delay is still evident.

It has been shown consistently that by establishing a vision, defining a mission, planning and setting goals, positively influences the performance of the institution.[19] It is urgent therefore that the mission statement, vision and values of the Seventh Day Adventist Church are known, understood and integrated by our pastors and members in local strategic planning; they should study it and publish it to be part of the actions of church life.

Our mission statement, as was approved by the Board of the General Conference on October 13, 2009 at the Annual Council in Silver Spring Maryland states:

> "The mission of the Seventh Day Adventist Church is to make disciples of all nations through the proclamation of the everlasting gospel in the context of the three angels' messages of Revelation 14 : 1-6, leading them to accept Jesus as personal Savior and to unite with his remnant church, and instructing them to serve the Lord and prepare for His soon return."

The document continues :

> "We carry out this mission under the guidance and training of the Holy Spirit, through the preaching, teaching, healing and discipleship."[20]

The purpose of the mission is to establish the reason for the company to disclose what it does, its main purpose is to provide direction. In fact as Ferrell et all, states:

> "Of all the components of the strategic plan, the mission is to be changed less frequently."[21]

It is the cornerstone of the strategic plan, if it changes, everything must change. For Adventist mission is clearly delineated in the word of God, so that could change your mission statement, to be a better way to express it, but not the mission itself, not its essence.

The vision for its part, is the box in which our preferred future is painted, its function is to provide inspiration, it evokes a picture that I have not yet seen but dream to reach in medium to long term.[22] It is rightly said that the vision defines the institution.[23] Values are the principles that unite us, in which we have agreed and ultimately shape our actions. They are indispensable for the harmonious and balanced development of any institution and more from the Church.

"You cannot achieve excellence if you do not have clear values and keep the firm conviction."[24]

It is impossible to talk about strategic planning in our various church levels, if these elements outlined previously are not sufficiently clear. Once set out, it is necessary some level of social research, remember that in the multitude of counselors there is wisdom.[25] It is not possible to achieve sound planning unless it is founded on research, and that's why, the concept of data mining has been popularized. In this new paradigm, the role of our Adventists universities is fundamental, they must work hand in hand with unions and local fields and take the lead in conducting relevant research to the local church community.

SWOT matrix

A simple and practical tool for raising and organizing information is the SWOT matrix, which corresponds to the acronym: Strengths, Weaknesses, Opportunities and Threats. Every institution has it internally with regard to fulfilling its mission, the achievement of the vision and the preservation of its values: strengths and weaknesses as well as externally: opportunities and threats.

As Jairo Amaya raises :

"There should be included key factors on the SWOT analysis related to the organization, markets, competition, financial resources, infrastructure, human resources, inventory, system marketing, distribution, research and development trends, social, economic and technological variables and competitiveness policies."[26]

For the Adventist church *Strengths* could be:

- Infrastructure: If you are attractive and strategically located.

- The quality of human resources, trained, responsive, sincere, active, united.

- The quality of worship and church programs, if they are inspiring.

Weaknesses could be:

- Deficient devotional habits of members and leaders of the congregation.
- The lack of attention to non-Adventist visitors.
- The lack of physical space.

Threats could be:

- Neighborhood Discontent (for e.g. parking)
- Crime
- Dissident groups

Opportunities could include:

- Frequent visitor attendance to the local congregation.
- Freedom of religion and worship.
- Good relations with the media.

Díaz de Santos comments on this delicate business assessment:

"The strengths and opportunities factors promote the achievement of objectives and the weaknesses and threats factors affect the achievement of objectives."[27]

Therefore as we name and classify SWOT indicators, it is important that a neat collection of information is done, for which it is vital to get the actors in the institutional activities and thus avoid biases and contradictions in the information.

In a Conference, custodians, teachers, pastors, departmental administrators, secretaries, a representative sample of the church members in general, should be consulted. In a church, the different segments of the congregation should be consulted.

Once data is collected, it is convenient to prioritize it, taking those points of highest impact, and proceed to evaluate them in order of importance within the project, in other words, if you list ten weaknesses we arrange them in order of importance and make sure not to repeat concepts. Once this process is through, you can proceed to building the matrix, which simply shows the internal and external conflict in order to generate alternative strategies.

Consider the following example:

Internal and External Analysis	Opportunities	Threats
Strengths	Potential	Risks
Weaknesses	Challenge	Limitations

This table shows that by correlating the opportunities offered by the environment with the internal strengths of the company you would reveal the potential and possibilities you will have on hand if strategic objectives were combined. By matching the environmental threats to my strengths, I am warned of the risks and so will leave it up the challenges and limitations. It is expected to generate attack strategies and institutional defense from this chart.

Consider also the following chart:

	Opportunities	Threats
Strengths	SO Strategies (Growth)	ST Strategies (Survival)
Weaknesses	WO Strategies (Survival)	WT Strategies (Escape)

The SO strategies aim to correlate the best opportunities in the environment with their own advantages, with the intention of growing the business outlined in the mission. If we have as one of our strengths: a comfortable temple with a prime location and we have the wonderful opportunity where we often get a good number of visitors we should be able to generate strategies aimed primarily to focus our programs and activities to accomplish the mission.

One idea could be to generate an inspiring Christ- centered worship and thus for the service of the mission, this will make all attendees remain in love and want to return, if instead they attend an impromptu meeting and sit through a monotonous program they may not be motivated to return.

The same logic is followed in the other case. The WO strategies seek to overcome internal weaknesses using the opportunities offered by the environment. The ST strategies try to address environmental threats, making good use of internal strengths.[28]

The WT strategies help to view alternatives of escape, given a situation of weakness and threat where the system is put at high risk. Other strategies such as SW, i.e. using one's strengths to address weaknesses are equally valuable and widely used.

These strategies should be split up into short, medium and long term objectives, which in turn must be achievable and measurable. A classic way is to make them operational by establishing the what, who, how, when and where, and in turn generating programs, schedules and budgets. It is further desirable to have a good system of assessment and accountability. It works!

Remember, salvation is a science, and science implies having a method; any method entails techniques, the techniques are not randomly chosen, but are part of a design, which follows a certain logic and structure. You can become a good seller depending only on the innate qualities, but you will always be more efficient if well educated in the art of marketing. To some extent the Evangelist is a salesman, offering ideas, wanting to conquer as many as possible for the kingdom of God.

Do not forget, we run with the horsemen! But no rider could or can match our Master, the great King who rides a white horse judging and fighting with justice.[29]

9th Evangelistic Principle

Structure strategic spiritual plans.

God wants us to integrate tools and techniques provided by him through science, and placed at the service of the great commission.

PRACTICAL IDEAS

1. Study and memorize the mission statement of the Seventh-day Adventist Church

2. Placed your local church's mission statement, vision and values in a visible place in your church.

3. Practice making a personal development plan for five years.

4. Make a SWOT exercise applying the tool to your local church

5. Promote in your local church a 5-year strategic plan to reach your community for Christ.

Aim today by the grace of Christ, to work in the vineyard of the Lord, in the order that the Lord of the vineyard requires!

Chapter 10

Flying Through the Sky

THE MISSION OF THE PREACHING ANGELS of Revelation is solemn and encompassing. They fly through the sky and with a loud voice, preach the everlasting gospel to every nation, tribe, tongue and people and illuminate the whole earth with their glory. Amazing! How could a small remnant achieve this? Obviously divine providence! But when considering how it is done, it is reasonable to think that the God of science and true author of progress, the only who is able to order 'let there be light', uses means to bless us.

If we notice well, what these preaching angels are doing is an aerial seeding. I must admit that I did not know that this type of agro-space resource was possible, but the truth is that the seeding aircraft, although somewhat unknown, is well documented and reported to be faster and more efficient and therefore less expensive than traditional methods.

While aerial reforestation is done through direct release of seeds from the air, as corn is traditionally sown, it is a real peculiar science because in order for the seed to be spread evenly and in the desired amount by surface, a diluted mixture must be prepared that takes into account the planned density of the seeds; it is also necessary to protect them from pest repellent and establish an optimal air operation logistic through a study of aerial photographs to define the boundaries and set forest inventory.

It is also necessary to design the flight plan with satellite coordinates on the computer, as well as taking into consideration the time and motion for planting and for refills of seed and fuel as needed. An estimated 410 hours of planting, flying and refueling operations is enough to reforest 120,000 hectares (296,526 acres) at a functional cost, incomparably less than with any other method.[1]

The printed page

I wonder, what about aerial sowing of the gospel? According to Ellen White, resources such as printing are among the advertising media represented by the flying angel, she states that it is from our publishing houses where the solemn message is given: Fallen, fallen is Babylon! And the great voice of the angel warns against the mark of the beast. She further states:

> "In a large degree through our publishing houses is to be accomplished the work of that other angel who comes down from heaven with great power and who lightens the earth with his glory."[2]

Do you ever wonder what made the Millerite movement so famous? Without a doubt, the printed page. For eight years, Miller worked as an itinerant preacher and a specialist in producing religious revivals. In December 1839, there was a very nice change when Joshua V. Himes (1805 - 1895), pastor of the Christian Connection, adopted its cause... an created Signs of the Times, the first of a few newspapers that he founded to spread the ideas of Miller. He also published more than forty books about the second coming in the space of five years.[3] Beyond that, Himes started the Midnight Cry publication in 1842 regarding the Millerite campaign in the large cities. He used to print ten thousand daily copies for several weeks. In 1842, six hundred thousands copies were distributed in five months alone.[4]

It was precisely Mrs. White whom after receiving the vision in Dorchester, Massachusetts, on November 1848, told her husband James:

> "I have a message for you. You must begin to print a little paper and send it out to the people... it was shown to me to be like streams of light that went clear round the world."[5]

Today, by the grace of God, the Seventh-day Adventist Church operates over fifty publishing houses around the world, has published in almost every known language, and thousands of canvassers spread these pages like autumn leaves, such as the tree of life is for the healing of the nations.

Only one of the SDA publishing houses, the South American, reported in 2012 an average use of 320 tons of paper monthly. Glory be to God![6]

In his time Martin Luther said: "The press is the latest gift given by God to mankind for evangelism."[7] We could say that when the fullness of the time had come, God sent the press of Johannes Gutenberg, which in 1455 inaugurated the western publishing industry with the printing of the Bible. After their contribution, the saying that "a drop of ink makes millions think and a pen is mightier than the sword", became true.

It is true that at times the press has been misused by producing books that should never have been printed, but although this slip belies the judgment of men, it does not diminish the great blessing represented by this instrument.

Observe the following declaration:

"The press is a powerful means to move the minds and hearts of the people. The men of this world seize the press, and make the most of every opportunity to get poisonous literature before the people. If men under the influence of the spirit of the world and of Satan, are earnest to circulate books, tracts, and papers of a corrupting nature, you should be more earnest to get reading matter of an elevating and saving character before the people."[8]

It is something to meditate on, isn't it true?

With great wisdom, Ellen G. White also said:

"Small tracts on the different points of Bible truth applicable to the present time should be printed in different languages and scattered where there is any probability that they would be read. God has placed at the command of His people advantages in the press, which, combined with other agencies, will be successful in extending the knowledge of the truth. Tracts, papers, and books, as the case demands, should be circulated in all the cities and villages in the land. Here is missionary work for all to engage in."[9]

What would be other instruments that would boost the knowledge of the truth? What about the radio, television, internet, social networking, audio books, tablets and applications for smart phones? Good! These sure are the latest gifts of God given to the preaching of the gospel.

As can be seen the real challenge is not to fly, but to link resources with people in their proper perspective, I think this detail catapulted the Millerite success. The idea is not to replace people but to empower them.

The expression "Here is missionary work for all to engage in" is true in the broadest sense, and it has never been so easy to publish as it is now! Forums, blogs, post, videos, tweets, are just some of the new forms of flying through the midst of space. With the democratization of knowledge the subject of publications is no longer exclusive to of our publishing houses, to some extent, every computer is a press and every Christian could be a writer or editor.

Adventist World Radio

Adventist World Radio (AWR)[10] is the official missionary radial branch of the Seventh-day Adventist Church and its mission is to convey the message of the second advent of Christ to groups more difficult to reach in the world in their own languages. Although the first Adventist radio station was established in the Emmanuel Missionary College in Michigan in 1923, just three years after the first radio broadcast in the United States,[11] this international radio initiative arises on the 1st of October,1971, in response to the challenge to reach people in communist countries of Europe.

AWR produce their programs in over 75 studios around the world and broadcast in some 90 languages daily from its own transmitter plant on the island of Guam and from rented transmitters in Europe, Africa, Madagascar, Taiwan, among other countries. This allows them to cover Africa, Europe, Latin America... and through satellite coverage to North America and northern Australia, basically almost everyone, though mostly in the Americas it is accomplished via FM affiliate stations webpages and podcast. In India alone, it is transmitted in ten languages and in the country of Myanmar (Burma) in eight languages, the great ethnic diversity in those places.

According to data available on its own web site in mid-2012, Adventist World Radio received more than 100,000 letters, phone calls and e-mails of radio listeners each year, which is a simple example of its scope. Each question or information requested by listeners receive a timely response and those who are interested in learning more about Christ are sent a guide for Bible studies and possible arrangements are made to bring them into contact with members of the church in their area who can provide spiritual help in their walk with God.[12]

As can be seen, it is through the AM, FM, short transmissions, satellite and internet wave, this glowing angel takes the message to the remotest nations, overcoming governmental, cultural, social and religious barriers. However, the main transmission is done through shortwave frequencies for their ability to travel long distances and penetrate many places with religious restrictions.

One of the main objectives of AWR is to share the gospel with the billions of people living in the countries of the 10/40 Window an area located between 10 and 40 degrees north latitude Ecuador, whose region covers North Africa, Middle East, much of Asia and the Pacific.

Meanwhile the dream is complete, in places like Morocco, Tibet, the Russian Federation, Ukraine and Moldova, countries like Ethiopia, Nigeria, Madagascar, India, Nepal, Vietnam, Democratic Republic of Congo, China, North Korea, Armenia and Georgia, among others, where they already hear the third angel's cry. It also works in the production of materials in local languages and local vernacular in places like Bhutan, Kazakhstan, Kyrgyzstan, Tajikistan, Uzbekistan, Turkmenistan, Azerbaijan, Albania, Israel, Namibia, Angola and new provincial / tribal languages in India, Ghana, Indonesia, Kenya, Senegal, etc.

It would be unfair to close the issue of the impact of Adventist radio without at least mentioning the names of H.M.S. Richards and Braulio Pérez Marcio. The first has been justly named the dean of the Adventist radio. He is globally known as the founder and first speaker in 1921 of the program that would later become 'The Voice of Prophecy'. The second served from 1942 to 1974 as speaker and director of La Voz de la Esperanza (The Voice of Prophecy), with his fruitful ministry impacting the lives of thousands and thousands of Hispanics.[13]

Seeing the wonders the Lord has done through the radio, we can also say that coming the fullness of time God sent Guillermo Marconi, Italian physicist, who in 1894 conducted the first tests of long distance radio transmission. Milton Peverini Garcia wrote:

> "There is no doubt that on a proper time God inspired Marconi for his invention to present the gospel with mighty power."[14]

Adventist television

From the first steps of mechanical television by John Baird (1926 - 1929) or electrical by Vladimir Zwuorikyn, and the following charms by Technicolor, cable television, the digital age, or the convergence of media, it has been more than evident its great evangelistic potential, but in reality its use has not been as strong as the radio.

However, Adventist television is becoming stronger and more professional every day. Church owned TV Channels like Hope, Novo Tempo, Esperanza TV, Loma Linda Broadcasting, and other Adventist channels are only the tip of the iceberg.

The program Faith for Today for example, first truly national religious broadcasting television in North America, was launched with the full sponsorship of the Seventh-day Adventist Church in May 1950 by William and Virginia Fagal. It is Written was founded in 1956 by George Vandeman and was the first religious program to air in color and the first to take advantage of satellite technology. Mark Finley replaced Vandeman in 1992; and this was just the beginning. Today Adventist TV programs can be seen on satellite, cable, Internet and many open channels in all inhabited continents.

Social medias and adventism

Social networks at its young age has played a significant and active role in all areas of society, including the activism of social rights, being mentioned even as a determining factor in the decline of some dictatorial regimes, especially in the so-called Arab Spring and no wonder, **Facebook,** the most visited social network in the world with 1.3 billion active users as of July, 2014 according to the world map of social networks. If Facebook regardless of a country would soon be the largest in the world, today would be surpassed only by China.

Other data from the same source and date Asia has 410 million users, 292 million in Europe, North America and Canada 204 million and the rest distributed in the other countries.[15] Meanwhile the popular Univision Network published in April 2012 that 61 % of Facebook users accessed their account daily, of which about half is done through cell phone or laptop tablet.[16]

Although **Twitter**, the social network of 140 characters, has a much smaller number of adherents, around 271 million users as of June 30, 2014, it is undoubtedly along with Facebook one of the most influential for the growing number of leaders and personalities that actively use it, and for the impressive influx from the cellular network.

A remarkable fact is that on December 12, 2012 at 12 am Pope Benedict XVI launched in all major languages of the world his first tweet, in which he said: "Dear friends, I join you with joy by Twitter. Thank you for your generous response. I bless you all from the heart." In this unprecedented act, came directly to your computer or mobile phone and quite possibly the hearts of a million followers, his newly created block of eight Twitter accounts, named @ Pontifex_es.[17]

YouTube, meanwhile, is the largest social platform in the world for videos and is also considered a social network used by brands, companies, ordinary users and artists among others. An estimated three billion hours of video in YouTube are viewed per month, with a mobility of more than a billion monthly visitors. There are many other social networks, but I will limit to these.

As for how the Adventist Church addresses the phenomenon, I refer to June 1, 2011 in Montego Bay, Jamaica the world's seventh forum where Global Adventist Internet Evangelism Network, (GAIN) was held, where approximately 90 Adventist representatives from all regions of the world gathered to share ideas and experiences on how to use the Internet for evangelism and edification of the church, as the leaders of Adventism are well aware of the evangelizing potential of social networks.

Interestingly all conferences dealt with the social networks especially in emerging media and how the church engages in mission effectively using social media strategies. The focus of the discussion was how the church can best use these social networks.

GAIN as a community of technophiles, evangelists and communicators discusses the creative use of internet technology. The community organized in 2004 is an initiative of the General Conference of Seventh-day Adventists, so the annual forum is hosted and sponsored by the Department of Communication at the world headquarters of the Church in cooperation with world divisions and interested lay people.

The 2012 Forum, the eighth of its kind, was conducted in Hong Kong with the participation of about 160 participants from all over the world and the ninth in the city of Dubai. In 2014 it took place in Baltimore, MD. Undoubtedly the subject raises great interest among leadership and much movement can be seen in their environment, and although it is still necessary to wait before evaluating results, the concern is that networks are progressing geometrically and we, in spite of our efforts are advance arithmetically, because the impact at church level is still very weak.

In any case even though receiving tweets from the world president would be great, I think the emphasis should be to train and inspire the great Adventist army to see the possibilities, and take evangelistic advantage of these resources and others in the near future, which with no doubt science will provide.

Institutional image

A subject of intense relevance for businesses today is institutional advertising, which aims to disseminate the image of the institution by promoting coordinated elements like name, staff quality, reputation, structure, values, mission and vision of the group. [18]

It is vital to succeed in establishing a favorable business attitude. Joaquín Sánchez and Teresa Pintado well refer to this matter by saying that "the corporate image is one of the key factors within organizations, but sadly not always cared for as it deserves."[19] It is important that the society knows what social projects the institution stands for, as well as anything that might tend to elevate the concept of citizens.

For Paul Capriotti, the projection of corporate image should be a fundamental object of the strategic planning of the company, with the deliberate intention of optimizing the whole idea with the subjects of the institution and its products, activities and behavior.[20]

On the other hand we must always remember that there is a close relationship between ideas about the company (its image) and visual elements that represent it (his identity). The image is generated by visual elements such as brand, color, typography, layout and personal forms, which together represent the corporate identity, and it tends to be regulated in an allusive manual purpose.

The Seventh-day Adventist Church also has its corporate identity manual, properly called 'Global Identity Standards Manual,' but it is very necessary to work in an intensive program of education and awareness in this respect as it is well suggested by advertisers. More dangerous than not having an identity is having it diffused.

Details such as the administrative stationary: letters, envelopes, business cards, printed forms, purchase tickets, catalogs, etc., architecture, presentation and organization of internal spaces, furniture, equipment, lighting, among many others cannot be overlooked when building a good image.

The denominational symbol of the Seventh-day Adventist Church

As highlighted in the Global Identity Standards, our denominational symbol consists of two parts: the logo, consisting of the words "Seventh-day Adventist Church," and the symbol. Both of them must be jealously guarded by the institution. Experts recommend rapid reaction to incorrect use of visual elements.

SEVENTH-DAY
ADVENTIST CHURCH

The manual warns that it is not enough to have an easily identifiable logo, it is necessary to ensure the consistent and correct use, attached to the manual parameters to avoid capricious application which project a blurry image, causing more harm than good. The institutional document expresses the meaning of every single detail of our symbols. I will transcribe the most relevant:

- **The Open Bible:** the Bible forms the base of the design and represents the biblical foundation of our beliefs. It is portrayed in a fully open position suggesting a full acceptance of God's word.

- **The Second Coming:** The lines at the top of the design suggest upward momentum symbolizing the resurrection and ascension to heaven at Christ's second coming, the ultimate focus of our faith.

- **The Flame:** This is the shape formed by three lines encircling an implied sphere. The lines represent the three angels of Revelation 14 circling the globe and our commission to take the gospel to the entire world. The overall shape forms a flame symbolic of the Holy Spirit.

- **The Cross:** The symbol of the cross, representing the gospel of salvation, is positioned in the center of the design to emphasize Christ's sacrifice, which is the central theme of the Adventist faith."[21]

It is significant also that the Bible, which represents the law, and the flame that represents the Spirit meet at the cross.

In conclusion, the remnant although small, since its inception has taken flying lessons, it is time to revisit the issue with the strength of the early years. The light should illuminate and the salt give flavor, the air force is not in doing tricks, but in defending the airspace.

10ᵗʰ Evangelistic Principle

Strengthen message presentation

Making use of wise use of technology, media, good strategy, and trained missionaries, we are challenged to consolidate the traditional media and move into the modern with the diligence that we started in the print media and radio.

PRACTICAL IDEAS

1. Explain to your church or small group the scope of the media group of the Adventist Church.

2. Probe what abilities your church could have to achieve a space on any media.

3. Consider with your church board the feasibility of joining evangelization through social networks.

4. Download from the internet the Global identity standards manual and plan to collaborate with your local church in such important aspects as the correct presentation of our logo and symbol.

Aim today by the grace of Christ to use all possible technological tools in evangelism at your local church or group of churches!

Chapter 11

The Foundation for Christian Effort

THE INFANTRY HAS HISTORICALLY been the main strength of armies but presently to go to battle without tactical forces supporting it would greatly limit its possibilities. The airborne forces have revolutionized the battlefield. Humanity remembers how the Israeli warplanes during the Six-day War (5 to June 5-10, 1967) made a surprise attack destroying Egyptian armies with its advanced tactics and air superiority.

Wikipedia, the free encyclopedia, has documented that the purpose of the German air force called Luftwaffe was to support the army, which greatly influenced his successes against Poland and France (1939-1940). Likewise, the Soviet Air Force was used primarily for tactical support for ground units.[1] However powerful air fleet can be it is not intended to replace the infantry but to support it; as effective bombing is, it is meaningless if there are no occupying forces.

The Seventh-day Adventist Church urges to actively link its air force with the infantry. It is true we have many television channels and publishers, but how are they linked with a foot soldier? Can those who are listening, reading or watching our programs, identify us at first sight when we knock the doors of their homes open to anyone? When the missionary opens his Bible in Exodus 20:1-17 and solemnly declares the Ten Commandments with its perpetual force will the spectators be reminded of hearing or reading the message from our mass media?

The previous chapter dealt with aerial force as the role of media in evangelization, this chapter is dealing with the fighting force on foot, the infantry and their role in the great conflict. The apostle Paul reminds us of a fight in which we must dress our feet with the preparation of the gospel of peace.[2] We wear the gospel as our boots to serve as instruments of Christ to crush the head of Satan. It is written: "The God of peace will soon crush Satan under your feet..."[3]

In the process of writing this book I exchanged an email with one executive of Adventist World Radio. The radio ministry was defined as a vanguard, entering places where missionaries cannot go, paving the way for a strong evangelism and forming congregations where conditions permit.

Interesting! The radio is not replacing but supporting. Air forces and infantry must work together, one army advancing in two fronts. As Christ's army we have much to improve in this aspect.

Convergence of methods

Media convergence has a major responsibility in the unprecedented development of the mass media. Instead of self-destruction they need to potentiate, rather than fight to interconnect. It is not about whether radio is replaced by television because the Internet outdates both. The idea is to move complementarily. It seems that Ithiel de Sola Pool, known as the prophet of convergence, was right. The digital era would revive the old media.

I wonder if there is a principle here that we can be apply to evangelism. Could we talk about convergence of methods? I think so. It is a matter of using them wisely to advance the kingdom of God. I am absolutely convinced that small groups are the basis of Christian effort, the foundation, the shoe, but not the whole effort.[4] Sadly, sometimes we spend more time discussing adequate methods rather than testifying.

Christ started his small group but also sent it out two by two to do personal evangelism, to heal, to teach and to evangelize publicly.

The light infantry has the task to venture into enemy's territory for exploration of complicated assault objectives during the war, but there is a mechanized infantry supporting infantry on foot. Both groups work for the army. Could not missionary teams explore the enemy territory and complicated assault objectives while small groups serve as safe battle tanks to protect soldiers?

God gave gifts to men, it is impossible to claim that those who have the gift of teaching will testify as much as the ones who have the gift of evangelism. In this matter we need unity in diversity, not uniformity. We gain little by having one method prevail over others, the night cometh when no man can work.

Consider these statements from Ellen White about gifts and other various methods:

1. "In connection with the proclamation of the message in large cities, there are many kinds of work that must be done by workers with varied gifts. Some have to work one way, some another."[5]

2. "The Lord desires His chosen servants to learn how to unite together in harmonious effort. It may seem to some that the contrast between their gifts and the gifts of a fellow laborer is too great to allow them to unite in harmonious effort; but when they remember that there are varied minds to be reached, and that some will reject the truth as it is presented by one laborer, only to open their hearts to God's truth as it is presented in a different manner by another laborer, they will hopefully endeavor to labor together in unity."[6]

3. "Means will be devised to reach hearts. Some of the methods used in this work will be different from the methods used in the work in the past; but let no one, because of this, block the way by criticism."[7]

4. "But let us not forget that different methods are to be employed to save different ones."[8]

5. "During the night of February 27 (1910), a representation was given me in which the unworked cities were presented before me as a living reality, and I was plainly instructed that there should be a decided change from past methods of working. For months the situation has been impressed on my mind, and I urged that companies be organized and diligently trained to labor in our important cities. These workers should labor two and two, and from time to time all should meet together to relate their experiences, to pray and to plan how to reach the people quickly, and thus, if possible, redeem the time."[9]

That is what I call convergence of methods!

I must emphasize that a good method can be used inappropriately as good soil can be planted wrong. It is personal duty to supervise the time of sowing. The Apostle Paul warned about using another foundation other than that of Jesus Christ:

> "For no one can lay any foundation other than the one already laid, which is Jesus Christ. If anyone builds on this foundation using gold, silver, costly stones, wood, hay or straw, their work will be shown for what it is, because the Day will bring it to light. It will be revealed with fire, and the fire will test the quality of each person's work. If what has been built survives, the builder will receive a reward. If it is burned up, the builder will suffer loss but yet will be saved — even though only as one escaping through the flames."[10]

Moreover, it is an administrative duty to evaluate the results, examine the development and real sustained growth in a period of time and not only the number of baptisms. It is also necessary to monitor levels of apostasy and analyze it with pastors and local churches, always in the interest of reducing it and shaping the edification of the Kingdom of Christ.

The missionary example of Jesus according to Ellen White

The following statements of Ellen White regarding the techniques, strategies and Jesus' evangelistic methods lead to the following conclusions:

Christ used several missionary *techniques* to attract people; the keyword here is to *attract*. I quote:

> "From Christ's methods of labor we may learn valuable lessons. He did not follow merely one method; in various ways He sought to gain the attention of the multitude, that He might proclaim to them the truths of the gospel."[11]

Christ used personal evangelism as his main *strategy* to evangelize. He knew that disciples are made individually, never in mass. His plan followed a scientific reasoning.

> "It is not preaching that is the most important; it is house-to-house work, reasoning from the Word, explaining the Word. It is those workers who follow the methods that Christ followed who will win souls for their hire."[12]

In a second statement Ellen White emphasizes:

"The Lord desires that His word of grace shall be brought home to every soul. To a great degree this must be accomplished by personal labor. This was Christ's method. His work was largely made up of personal interviews. He had a faithful regard for the one-soul audience. Through that one soul and message was often extended to thousands."[13]

Christ used one method, a standardized procedure to disciple people. His plan followed a scientific reasoning. If we take these steps we will have the same results, it is no coincidence, it is celestial science:

"Christ's method alone will give true success in reaching the people. The Saviour mingled with men as one who desired their good. He showed His sympathy for them, ministered to their needs, and won their confidence. Then He bade them, 'Follow Me'" [14]

Christ used a method of establishing new congregations. The same also obeyed scientific reasoning:

"This was the way the Christian Church was established. Christ first selected a few persons and bade them follow Him. They then went in search of their relatives and acquaintances, and brought them to Christ. This is the way we are to labor. A few souls brought out and fully established on the truth will, like the first disciples, be laborers for others."[15]

Urban evangelism principles in the light of the writings of Ellen G. White

Below are some highly relevant evangelistic principles outlined to reach the cities, drawn from the writings of Ellen G. White. Other principles of great importance are not presented here, but are part of another section.[16]

1. **Our houses should be located in the purest possible place.**

   - Following the example of Enoch, by going to evangelize the cities, we locate our own homes in the purest possible place. (Manuscript Releases, vol.10, p.241, par.1)

   - "More and more, as wickedness increases in the great cities, we shall have to work them from outpost centers." (RH, September 27, 1906, par.18)

   - "In no uncertain words the Lord has warned us not to establish large institutions in the cities." (RH July 5, 1906, par. 7).

2. We also have to establish our homes strategically

- Jesus chose Capernaum for its strategic location (Matthew 4:13). It was a place of great traffic and where I could meet people from all nations and conditions, this ensured that lessons were carried many homes and places. The strategy of Christ involved the most tactical possible place. This is a very important detail to consider. (Testimonies for the Church, vol.9, p.121)

- "At such a time as this, the people who are seeking to keep the commandments of God should look for retired places away from the cities. Some must remain in the cities to give the last note of warning, but this will become more and more dangerous to do. Yet the truth for today must come to the world..." (Manuscript 85, 1908)

3. Health and age are vital factors to consider when sending missionaries

- "Feeble or aged men and women should not be sent to labor in unhealthful, crowded cities." (Letter 168, 1909).

4. The evangelization of the cities must be done urgently

- "If we do not take up this work in a determined manner, Satan will multiply difficulties which will not be easy to surmount. We are far behind in doing the work that should have been done in these long-neglected cities. " (Medical Ministry, pp.301,302)

- "In a little while from this we shall be unable to work with the freedom that we now enjoy. Terrible scenes are before us, and what we do we must do quickly." (Manuscript 53, 1909)

- "I was shown that we do not at the present time move as fast as the opening providence of God leads the way." (Life Sketches of Ellen G. White, p.209, par.2)

5. The wickedness of the great cities should not discourage us

- "God's messengers in the great cities are not to become discouraged over the wickedness, the injustice, the depravity, which they are called upon to face while endeavoring to proclaim the glad tidings of salvation." (Prophets and Kings, p.277, par.2)

- "Satan is busily at work in our crowded cities... That men may not take time to meditate... leads them into a round of gayety and pleasure-seeking, of eating and drinking. He fills them with ambition to make an exhibition that will exalt self." (Manuscript 139, 1903)

- "We should cherish hatred of sin, but pity and love for the sinner... Every day the probation of some is closing. Every hour some are passing beyond the reach of mercy." (Patriarchs and Prophets, p.140, par.1)

- "All through our large cities God has honest souls who are interested in what is truth." (Manuscript 29, 1909)

6. Urban evangelization is a responsibility of all of us

- "The ordained ministers alone are not equal to the task of warning the great cities." (The Acts of the Apostles p.158, par.3)

- "The work of the gospel is to be carried by means of our liberality as well as by our labors." (Manuscript 7, 1908)

7. Sensationalism and controversy are disruptive for the work of evangelizing the cities

- "It is enough to present the truth of the Word of God to the people. Startling notices are detrimental to the progress of His work... "(Letter 176, 1903)

- "It is of little use to try to reform others by attacking what we may regard as wrong habits. Such effort often results in more harm than good. In His talk with the Samaritan woman, instead of disparaging Jacob's well, Christ presented something better... This is an illustration of the way in which we are to work. We must offer men something better than that which they possess..." (The Ministry of Healing, pp.156, 157)

8. Teaching and healing should never be separated

- "In the work of the gospel, teaching and healing are never to be separated." (The Ministry of Healing, p.140)

9. God will raise up workers chosen for the work in the cities

- "In our large cities the message is to go forth as a lamp that burneth. God will raise up laborers for this work, and His angels will go before them. Let no one hinder these men of God's appointment. Forbid them not. God has given them their work." (Review and Herald, September 30, 1902)

- "There should be no delay in this well-planned effort to educate the church members. Persons should be chosen to labor in the large cities who are fully consecrated and who understand the sacredness and importance of the work." (Testimonies for the Church, vol.9, p.119)

10. Each city requires special studies and particular strategies

- "The situation in all the large cities must be studied, that the truth may be given to all the people." (Letter 88, 1910)

- "Men should study what needs to be done in the places that have been neglected. The Lord has been calling our attention to the neglected multitudes in the large cities, yet little regard has been given to the matter." (RH November 11, 1909, par.16)

11. The evangelization of the cities will fill the church with spiritual and material blessings

- "The work in the cities is the essential work for this time, and is now to be taken hold of in faith. When the cities are worked as God would have them, the result will be the setting in operation of a mighty movement such as we have not yet witnessed." (Medical Ministry, p.331, par.3)

- "As we do this work, we shall find that means will flow into our treasuries, and we shall have means with which to carry on a still broader and more far-reaching work." (Manuscript 53, 1909)

- "All the united converted agencies are to combine in one, and the law of cooperation is the great one work in reciprocal influence." (Letter 183, 1901)

- "Prosperity will never attend these churches until the individual members shall be closely connected with God, having an unselfish interest in the salvation of their fellow men. Ministers may preach pleasing and forcible discourses, and much labor may be put forth to build up and make the church prosperous; but unless its individual members shall act their part as servants of Jesus Christ, the church will ever be in darkness and without strength." (Testimonies for the Church, vol.8, p.285, par.2)

- "The lack of effort to plant the standard of truth in the cities of America has brought about a condition of things in which the consuming is larger than the producing..." (Letter 20, 1903)

12. God will not accept excuses for the negligence to evangelize the cities

- "The churches now in different parts of Greater New York are to feel their sacred, God-given responsibilities.... God will not tolerate any longer the spirit that has been controlling matters in our New York churches." (AU Gleaner, January 8, 1902)

- "Rather than have the work in New York interrupted, I would hire money and pay interest on it, in order to carry the work forward." (Letter 141, 1901)

13. Once the truth is presented as it is in Jesus, whoever rejects it is responsible for their own fate

- "The door that is open to the missionary will also be open to the opposer of truth. But if the truth is presented as it is in Jesus, the hearers are responsible for its rejection." (RH July 2, 1895, par.2)

14. The truth must shine in as many places as possible

- "The enemy would be rejoiced to see the grand, saving truth for this time confined to a few places." (Letter 168, 1909)

- "Instead of having mammoth camp meetings in a few localities, more good would be done by having smaller meetings in many places." (Manuscript 3, 1899)

- "The presentation of Christ in the family, by the fireside, and in small gatherings in private houses, is often more successful in winning souls to Jesus than are sermons delivered in the open air, to the moving throng, or even in halls or churches." (Gospel Workers 1915, 193)

15. Open urban evangelism schools wherever you want to seriously evangelize

- "More attention should be given to training and educating missionaries with a special reference to work in the cities." (Letter 34, 1892)

- "A well-balanced work can be carried on best in the cities when a Bible school for the training of workers is in progress while public meetings are being held." (Gospel Workers 1915, 364)

- "Every member of the church should learn how to communicate light to others who sit in darkness. Let everyone watch for souls 'as they that must give account.'" (RH June 11, 1895, par.2)

16. Conquering the homes for Christ is an indispensable mission

- "The Lord has presented before me the work that is to be done in our cities. The believers in these cities are to work for God in the neighborhood of their homes." (Testimonies for the Churches, vol.9, p.128)

- "Every method by which access may be gained to the homes

of the people must be tried; for the messenger must become acquainted with the people." (The Bible Echo – May 21, 1894, par.1)

17. The scientific methods applied will enhance evangelization work

- "Men in responsible positions should improve continually. They must not anchor upon an old experience, and feel that it is not necessary to become scientific workers." (Testimonies for the Church, vol.4, p.93)

18. The message must be simple, yet strategic and powerful

- "The Lord is speaking to his people at this time, saying, *Gain an entrance into the cities,* and proclaim the truth in simplicity and in *faith."* (RH January 18, 1912, par.5)

- "The greatest care is needed in dealing with these souls. Be always on guard. Do not at the outset press before the people the most objectionable features of our faith, lest you close the ears of those to whom these things come as a new revelation." (Manuscript 44, 1894)

- We need to capture the attention of the audience by presenting the truth as it is in Jesus. First and most important is to soften and subdue the soul presenting our Lord Jesus Christ as our Savior who forgives us and it is not made through long and elaborate speeches but through discussions short and precise. (Manuscript 3, 1899)

- "The truth for this time is to be proclaimed. A decided testimony is to be borne. And the discourses are to be so simple that children can understand them." (Testimonies for the Church, vol.8, p.184, par.3)

19. The work of intercession for the cities must be persistent

- "Abraham asked not once merely, but many times... he continued until he gained the assurance that if even ten righteous persons could be found in it, the city would be spared." (Patriarchs and Prophets, p.139, par.3)

The challenges are numerous in this area as it can be seen:

- Integrate air force with infantry,
- Educate about the convergence of methods and
- Integrate principles of urban evangelism reflected in the Bible and the prophetic writings of Ellen White into our strategic plans.

God has made ample provision to show the way, so: let us follow it.

11th Evangelistic Principle

Link mass media with local churches more efficiently

We must converge the different techniques, strategies and methods Christ left us, and then, submit the results to short, medium and long term evaluation.

PRACTICAL IDEAS

1. Subscribe to the missionary magazine of the church and become a volunteer from the printed page.

2. Take an afternoon and help your neighbors to tune the Adventist radio or TV channel received in your community.

3. Multiply your church in small groups and then into missionary teams.

4. Discuss how your church can converge different evangelistic media, before they are dead.

5. Establish a small group in your home.

6. Establish the missionary teams in your church or small group.

Aim today by the grace of Christ to be a faithful soldier in the army of Christ! Remember, to testify is not a personal gift, but a commandment of God to His people.

Chapter 12

With Such An Army

FOR FORTY YEARS MOSES instructed Joshua[1], Naomi discipled Ruth, Elijah to Elisha, Mordecai to Esther and the apostle Paul to Titus and Timothy whom he called true children in the faith[2]. These examples show how God integrates different generations in favor of the plan of salvation. We know that this kind of agreement to blend workforce increases the potential but also the complexity to lead and manage.

It is wonderful to see how the Bible's leaders instructed the youth. It was not simply to pass the torch and stand aside, but to identify, to disciple and empower. There is not doubt that combining youth with experience is the closest strategy to perfection in human terms. It is not in vain that popular wisdom recommends putting together a new ox with an old one.

I think that Ellen White visualized an outlined concept of youth and their coaching staff when she wrote:

> "With such an army of workers as our youth, rightly trained, might furnish, how soon the message of a crucified, risen, and soon-coming Saviour might be carried to the whole world! ..." [3]

It is God's plan that experienced men and women educate and encourage the youth. As Ellen G. Write stated: "There is no class that can achieve greater results for God and humanity than the young." [4]

Generation glance

A group of individuals that possess equivalent age and live in the same period, having similar characteristics and social context, values, beliefs and behavioral traits is called generation. Obviously this whole issue of generations is multifaceted and heavily permeated by the culture and levels of development, however day by day the globalization and technological process blur more the social and cultural boundaries, the generational characteristics are more precise and coincident. In the last hundred years five generations are recognized:

1. **The silent generation** lived during the first half of the XX century. It is located by others between 1917 and 1939 and beyond in Latin America and other countries with similar characteristics. They are defined as workers and keepers of the traditional systems through institutions such as family, school and church, exercising great control over the individual's life.

2. **The Baby-Boomers** are recognized as the second generation of the century. There is no consensus because some locate them between 1940 and 1961 and others between 1946 and 1964. They were marked by the arrival of man on the moon and the Vietnam War, defined as socially liberal and radical in its challenge to the establishment. It is the generation of the Rock and Roll, excesses and the beginning of women's liberation in some ways.[5]

3. **The Generation X** are the children of the baby boomers, often located between 1962 and 1980. They are known as the lost generation, natural product of cynicism and the incongruity of their parents. The Xs were faced with an increasingly technological society, but eclectic and lacking of ideals, many were raised in nurseries and others for the TV. They prefer to live in urban centers, are highly egocentric and compulsive buyers. They are characterized by their lack of commitment and intolerance. Many of them are considered digital immigrants. The X's parenting has a more active role with their grandkids, because of the increasing divorces and single parenthood.

4. **The Generation Y** is the generation of the late XX century, frequently placed between 1982 and 1995 or 1982 and 2002 according to the Demographics and Population Generation Trends[6]. They are the generation of the Gulf War, the rise of the Internet and telecommunications, including the cable television and answering machines; are considered digital natives and is often referred as *Millennials*. This generation is open to controversial issues and address complex problems as well as being part of "blended families" and a single parent.[7]

5. **The Generation YouTube or WEB Generation** comes in the beginning of the XXI century (also called Net Generation) and as the name implies they integrate technology as part of their vital organs, most of them are disrespectful, why they have been called the generation of petty tyrants. Generally they are children of the X or the Y. Many can speak two languages but do not know what to say in these two languages; work with multiple computer windows open and believe that everything in life is handled the same way: the love, the church and society. Finally, they do not want superiors but much less if they do not handle computers, have low self-esteem and very little respect for the world around.

Generation's renewal and evangelizing cities

The Church of Christ is committed to all generations, its message should reach not only every nation, but to every generation and in every generation they must be well balanced and judicious integrating the leadership.

Traditionally, a generation's renewal is linked to the replacement of tired troops in the war field, but I would like to move to the sports' world to illustrate my point. There are several types of relay races including: orienteering, swimming, skiing, biathlon and ice skating, but let's concentrate on the relays in athletics in which a runner travels a certain distance then the next runner continues carrying a rigid tube called baton[8] and so on until the race distance is completed.

This is a nice metaphor for several reasons. First, the one carrying the baton as the one who came before are both part of the team; no runner disappears from the stage and goes away from the race because the defeat or victory belongs to everyone, as long as one runs the team runs.

Second, you need to pass the baton to someone on the team. The *baton* is not given to a spectator who delights from the stands but to another vigorous runner. Paul told Timothy, "Meditate upon these things; give thyself wholly to them; that thy profiting may appear to all"[9]. John Stott commenting on this passage relates that Timothy was committed to show constant progress and improvement, people should see what he was and what he was becoming.[10]

Possibly in some places there are adult leaders who desperately want to pass the baton but cannot see the advantage of the youth and fear that the vision will perish in their hand. The years strike them and the mission becomes adrift. Evidently they did not find a takeover for the leader they did not form. The exercise of an empowering leadership is urgent in our churches!

Ellen G. White wrote:

"Young men should be qualifying themselves for service by becoming familiar with other languages, that God may use them as mediums through which to communicate His saving truth to those of other nations. ... If they are economical of their time they can improve their minds and qualify themselves for more extended usefulness."[11]

She also admonished:

"The Lord calls upon our youth to labor as canvassers and evangelists, to do house-to-house work in places that have not yet heard the truth. ... One of the very best ways in which young men can obtain a fitness for the ministry is by entering the canvassing field. Let them go into towns and cities to canvass for the books which contain the truth for this time. In this work they will find opportunity to speak the words of life, and the seeds of truth they sow will spring up to bear fruit."[12]

The generation's renewal should flow naturally in our churches but it is not about replacing the old generation with the new like a car's tires replacement as the law of denial in the dialectical materialism proposes. Rather it is written "You shall rise before the gray headed... and fear your God: I am the Lord."[13]

It is sin to try to corner wisdom!

If we follow the advice and example of the Word of God, we will have a dynamic, wise, fresh and new church. I still remember the day my father told me: "Manuel, now your mother and I will do whatever our sons ask." I immediately replied, "No!" And he calmly said, "We do voluntarily, I know that the ranks are from one generation to the next." I told them, "The ranks will be yours while you live." Today we continue making decisions as a family, in consensus, our parents in their irreplaceable place and we as sons in our proper one.

Third, both the transfer of the *baton* and the renewal obey certain rules and principles. If you pass the baton improperly you are disqualified, if you run more or less the distance you should, then you are disqualified. It is important to know that the runners are not equally fast, so the order of a team of four runners should be: second fastest, third fastest, slowest, and then fastest. What needs to be ensured is that every runner is in his right place when the time demands.

Young people are fast. The apostle John wrote:

"I have written to you, young men, because you are strong, and the word of God abides in you, and you have overcome the wicked one." [14]

However often this force needs to be educated and guided.

Experience tends to sharpen the spiritual discernment. Joshua in his innocence said to Moses when they were descending from the mountain, "*There is* a noise of war in the camp." And Moses said, "*It is* not the noise of the shout of victory, nor the noise of the cry of defeat, *but* the sound of singing I hear."[15] Joshua was learning how to discern and became a great leader.

Paul recognized a special gift of administration in Titus and proposed to develop him entrusting the ecclesiastical organization of the church in the Island of Crete:

"For this reason I left you in Crete, that you should set in order the things that are lacking, and appoint elders in every city as I commanded you."[16]

If we want to develop youth leadership, we must give them opportunities. I was pastor of a large church district at 23 years old.

I used to ask my local leaders why we could not integrate elders and deacons of 18 years old. The church of the future is here!

Experience and discretion from adults and strength from the youth are needed to evangelize cities. Paul said to Timothy:

> "Let no one despise your youth, but be an example to the believers in word, in conduct, in love, in spirit, in faith, in purity." [17]

The reality is that is difficult to understand the changes taking place in society unless they are contemplated through the generational lens. Young people understand the language of modernity, technology and society. If we want to reach the cities young people have to take their place! The *Web Generation* hardly progress if they do not see their parents or older siblings in the front chain of command to mention one example.

In the business world the younger generation continues to climb to the summit of leadership at a gradually rapid pace, the reason we can see today most renowned local and multinational corporations a new generation of managers with completely different priorities and motivations in the ways to communicate, leadership styles and technology opinion. The church cannot be left behind! If a man can be president of the United States at age 42 – talking about Theodore Roosevelt – or 43 in the case of John F. Kennedy, what is the position that cannot be occupied?

The urban church will arise a new generation of leaders. This is the time to intentionally do that, the future of the cities will depend on a new generation of leaders.[18]

The role of children

A squad of the army of Christ that we should pay attention is our children. They have advantages and a special grace that few dare to resist. Commenting Gaussen as he prodigiously preached the message of the Second Advent in Geneva, he decided to start with the children expecting to reach the parents through them.

Ellen G. White collects his testimony in these words:

> "I determined therefore to go to the youngest. I gather an audience of children; if the group enlarges, if it is seen that they listen, are pleased, interested, that they understand and explain the subject, I am sure to have a second circle soon, and in their turn, grown people

will see that it is worth their while to sit down and study. When this is done, the cause is gained."[19]

Their success was overwhelming and soon that church was filled of concerned parents and guardians that curiously came to receive the bread of the Word. Ellen G. White continues with the following shocking statements:

1. "In many places where the preachers of the Lord's soon coming were thus silenced, God was pleased to send the message, in a miraculous manner, through little children. As they were under age, the law of the state could not restrain them, and they were permitted to speak unmolested.

2. "... Some of them were not more than six or eight years of age; and while their lives testified that they loved the Saviour, and were trying to live in obedience to God's holy requirements, they ordinarily manifested only the intelligence and ability usually seen in children of that age. When standing before the people, however, it was evident that they were moved by an influence beyond their own natural gifts.

3. "It was God's will that the tidings of the Saviour's coming should be given in the Scandinavian countries; and when the voices of His servants were silenced, He put His Spirit upon the children, that the work might be accomplished. When Jesus drew near to Jerusalem attended by the rejoicing multitudes that, with shouts of triumph and the waving of palm branches, heralded Him as the Son of David, the jealous Pharisees called upon Him to silence them;... but the children in the temple courts afterward took up the refrain, and, waving their branches of palm, they cried: 'Hosanna to the Son of David!' Matthew 21:8-16. When the Pharisees, sorely displeased, said unto Him, 'Hearest Thou what these say?' Jesus answered, 'Yea; have ye never read, Out of the mouth of babes and sucklings Thou hast perfected praise?'"[20]

Just as in the time of the first advent of Christ God worked through the children, He will also intervene through them to proclaim the message of His second advent.

(See twelfth evangelistic principle on next page)

12th Evangelistic Principle

Need to develop leadership in which each generation fulfills its mission efficiently.

While doing this, it is necessary to identify, disciple and encourage the next generation of runners. Great challenge!

PRACTICAL IDEAS

1. Organize youth leadership training schools to all church levels.

2. Integrate teens and youth in all departments of the local churches.

3. Each adult should choose at least one young and lead him or her according to the biblical style.

4. To study deeper the issues of generational characteristics and explain to young people how to build a biblical generation to choose the good and discard the bad.

5. To foster meetings and conversations between the boys and girls and the old men and women.

Aim today by the grace of Christ to integrate as many young people as you can in your local church leadership!

Chapter 13

The Upper Class and Special Groups

THE TERM 'HIGH CLASS' applies to the group of people with more wealth and power in the society. Although there is no general consensus on their limits and specific characteristics, the following inclusion criteria are recognized:

- A maximum economic prosperity in society of reference;
- A high degree of economic influence, primarily associated with the management of large companies;
- A respectable political and social position.[1]

These features seem interesting, because when analyzing over a hundred biblical references the Strong concordance lists for the term riches, I note that in essence the various terms are associated with three core areas:

- **Possessions, property**, according to the Hebrew term Recúsh (רְכֻשׁ) mentioned in Genesis 15:14, which states: "But I will punish the nation they serve as slaves, and afterward they will come out with great possessions."

- **Power, means, ability**, according to the Hebrew term KJáil (חַיִל) used in Psalm 62:10, which relates: "Do not trust in extortion or put vain hope in stolen goods; though your riches increase, do not set your heart on them."

- **Splendor, glory, majesty, honor**, according to the Hebrew term kabod (כָּבֹד) mentioned in Genesis 31:1, which reads: "Jacob heard that Laban's sons were saying,"Jacob has taken everything our father owned and has gained all this wealth from what belonged to our father."

Sociological considerations

Most definitions in the field of sociology are based on the theoretical framework of Max Weber, focused on the interaction of the variables: wealth, power and prestige. For Weber, society is stratified along three parallel dimensions: economic, political and social and particularly the economic which basic indicators are the market position and ability to access certain assets and opportunities. Others rely on the theory of Karl Marx, for whom the classes are defined primarily in terms of the social relations of production. Here, raw possession and use of manufacturing resources used to produce other goods.[2]

There is also the functionalist perspective, considered the third classical approach of social stratification. For Talcott Parsons, one of its leading exponents, moral evaluation is the central criterion governing stratification. Other factors to consider are: status, unit of kinship, cultural traits and finally the personal qualities, achievements, possessions, authority and power.[3]

Modern proposals for social groupings

Of the various groups of classes that exist, I quote the one developed by Mora and Araujo, from the construction of the index of social economic status (NES) in Argentina, which its advocates say, moves over the debate between the primacy in the production process and consumption position, establishing a new vision of stratification from the groups that manage access to certain goods.

The analyzed index used six categories grouped into three classes: the affluent (comprising the sub segments: High -high AB- C1, with 7% of the population and the High C2 with 11%), middle class (comprising sub segments: Medium-High C3, with 25 % of the population and the medium -low D1 with 22%) and the lower classes (comprising the sub segments : Low D2, with 28% of the population and low -low E, with 7%).[4]

Another important study is Portes and Hoffman, focusing on class structures in Latin America, grouped from the Social Panorama of Latin America 1999-2000 study conducted by ECLAC in eight countries of the region: Brazil, Chile, Colombia, Costa Rica, El Salvador, Mexico, Panama and Venezuela.

Stratification of social classes

Dominant
Capitalists, executives, managers and employees of elite

Intermediate
The petty bourgeoisie (independent professionals and entrepreneurs and directly supervised staff) and non-manual formal proletariat: clerical and technical employees with vocational training

Subordinate
Fueled by the informal proletariat, including wage workers without contracts, street vendors and unpaid family workers.

It is noteworthy that the mean percentage of the ruling class is only 8.56 % and if you only consider the Capitalists, the percentage would drop to only 1.55%.[5] According to Camilo Sembler As quoted in his social stratification of social classes, only 6.2% belongs to the ruling class, 44.3 % to 45.9 % intermediate and the informal proletariat.[6]

The critique to these efforts are based in the inconsistency between many of the studies and social perceptions. There is a large gap between intra - classes, doubts about the reliability of the sources and lack of consensus in the methods of analysis, which has forced new analytical dimensions, especially related to issues such as consumer education, lifestyle characteristics and possession of a certain degree of cultural capital.

According to Pierre Bourdieu social classes should not be

analyzed primarily from individuals or their inherent character-istics. It is more accurate to analyze them from their position in the network of social relations that can be defined as class struc-ture.[7] That's why he proposes to distinguish between the terms: class status and class position.

Upper and medium strata

For missionary purposes, it is more convenient to speak of upper stratum, eliminating the class condition, and there-fore, any feature that integrates the combination of occupational, labor, social and educational criteria, and focus strictly on the level of per capita household income. To line up the actual upper class would limit us to a very small group, thus if we focus on the upper class it is not the same to talk about the high class and the high stratum.

Speaking of Zaccheus, Ellen White relates:

"'The chief among the publicans,' Zacchaeus was a Jew, but detested by his countrymen. His rank and wealth were the reward of a calling they abhorred, and which was regarded as another name for injus-tice and extortion."[8]

Clearly Zacchaeus would hardly be accepted as part of the upper class[9], composed of the refined and 'ultra honest': Attor-neys, Romans, Tribunes, Elders and the High Priest. Although he had money, his profession was discredited. What cannot be denied is the fact that he belonged to an affluent socioeconomic strata.

Get to work!

To evangelize any social group or population segment, it is necessary to review the specific details of what the Bible says regarding how people are saved. Since at the foot of the cross there are no social classes, we have all sinned, we all fall short and we all need the same plan of redemption, Calvary is a good place to start thinking. [10]

First, salvation is by grace. Paul is blunt: "For by grace are ye saved through faith, and that not of yourselves: it is the gift of

God."[11] All human beings need the same remedy, Grace: a gift of divine manufacturing that comes through faith.[12] Faith, in turn, comes by hearing the word of Christ.[13] That is, the gift of grace is received in the heart; the person should come in contact with the Word, as Jesus said referring to them "... They testify of Me."[14] To hear it, or come in contact with the Word in any way is essential for salvation.

Paul speaking to the Romans in the context that "everyone who calls on the name of the Lord shall be saved" reflects:

> "But how can they call on whom they have not believed in? And how shall they believe in whom they have not yet heard of? And how can they hear without a preacher?"[15]

It is a chain of cause and effect reasoning: preach, hear, believe, invoke, and it is precisely here that we Christians go into action, whom the Holy Scriptures call Ambassadors.[16]

Personally, I think the basic reason why we don't get close to the middle and upper socioeconomic strata is not because they reject the gospel, or do not want to hear, (it is a special genre that's for sure) but the first barrier is that there is no one to preach, so they do not hear, do not believe, do not call on, do not receive grace, are not baptized and are not candidates for the Heavenly Home.

When Philip asked the eunuch Aristocrat, "Do you understand what you read?" He answered "How can I understand if no one explains it to me ?" He invited Philip to come up and sit with him.[17] Undoubtedly many wealthy people would be saved, if only someone would explain the scriptures to them.

Paul, in his chain of reasoning, also asks, How will they preach unless they are sent? As can be seen it is a whole sequence, the idea of being sent evokes a plan, a focus, an intention and that is exactly what we need as a church, intentionality; also orienting ourselves toward the middle and upper social strata.

Perhaps the country where we have least missionaries is called upper class, or rather *upper strata*. Allow me to make a secondary application, but an objective one. Matthew 24:14 says that the gospel must be preached to all nations (εθνεσιν), people, race, nation, ethnicity. The idea is that the gospel should reach anyone. Therefore, I think that the spirit of the text has not altered by viewing the rich as a special breed to which it is also necessary to achieve.

Jesus told his disciples: "... Truly I tell you, it is hard for someone who is rich to enter the kingdom of heaven."[18], But in the same context exclaims "With man this is impossible, but with God all things are possible."[19] The rich have against them the worries of this life[20] and the deceitfulness of riches choke the Word.[21] Riches are undoubtedly competing with Christ for the lordship of the Heart. It is the law of heaven that we cannot serve God and riches.[22] The rich young ruler illustrates this point well.[23]

Another thing to consider is that the rich usually arrive late, or at night as did Nicodemus, have more fear than common people.[24] Ellen White wrote about him:

"He would not go to Jesus by day, for this would make him a subject of remark. It would be too humiliating for a ruler of the Jews to acknowledge himself in sympathy with the despised Nazarene."[25]

Naaman proclaim right after he was healed: "... Indeed, now I know that there is no God in all the earth..." or "for your servant will no longer offer either burnt offering or Behold, now I know there is no God in all the earth... "Or"... For from now on your servant will not offer burnt offering or sacrifice to any gods, but the LORD." Recalling his ties to the state, he confessed:

"Yet in this thing may the Lord pardon your servant: when my master goes into the temple of Rimmon to worship there, and he lean son my hand, and I bow down in the temple of Rimmon- when I bow down in the temple of Rimmon, may the Lord please pardon your servant in this thing."[26]

The amazing and sobering is that the prophet of the Lord did not rebuke or accuse him, he was empathetic and having fulfilled his part he instructed him to the manifold grace of God. "... And he said, Go in peace."

Joseph of Arimathea was a disciple of Jesus, but secretly, for fear of the Jews.[27] These two words hardly walk together, if a disciple is a follower, how can you follow in secret?

The rich sometimes break our schemes, their interests and social and political influence can be disconcerting to many of our brothers and sisters, but if we are patient, in their time they will come out of hiding and come to the front of the battle, as did

Joseph asking the body of Christ boldly to Pilate[28]. The same can be said about Nicodemus.[29]

A practical example

The Southeastern Conference of Seventh-day Adventists in the Dominican Republic launched a project of evangelization in six points of its territory, most by middle strata, in which there was no Adventist presence.

The plan took place when eleven youth pastors, divided into pairs began to knock on the doors of the houses, doing surveys, distribute literature, etc... Others preferred to be aided with personal references by Adventists gathered elsewhere, but who had family or friends in the evangelized place. The truth is that all, by the grace of God, and with the collaboration of Adventists of the closest communities were able to establish the proposed congregations before the expiry of the prescribed period, which was one year.

Even in places that were considered impenetrable with the luxurious housing and elusive of its inhabitants, and in spite of other daunting factors such as crime, people opened their doors, and even in places where the ministers of God were not initially received, after the neighbors saw that others had received them safely themselves, also received them at home.

Small groups were established in designated places; they taught finance and health classes; gave evangelistic campaigns, shared dozens of books and distributed literatures which were Christ centered, and alluded to the eight natural remedies. There were also baptisms and organized churches. Therefore, if you decide to visit you will meet new Adventist congregations in: El Rosal II, Paco I, Brisas, Vista Hermosa and Máximo Gómez. If they are sent, some will hear and believe. To God be the glory!

Who will go for us?

"I heard the voice of the Lord saying, Whom shall I send, and who will go for us? Then said I, Here am I, send me."[30]

I hear the Lord asking the same question... Who will go for us? You may want to respond and be wondering: Can I come? Or do I have to be rich to evangelize the rich?

If we follow the principles of the Bible it will be very easy to take the gospel to every nation, kindred, tongue and people. In fact the universality of the message is as categorical as it is imperative.[31] The answer is Yes, you can go. God blesses in a special way anyone who will wholeheartedly come to him with the intention of being his instrument and is subject to the prophetic standards.

In his first letter to the Corinthians Paul writes:

"Brothers and sisters, think of what you were when you were called. Not many of you were wise by human standards; not many were influential; not many were of noble birth. But God chose the foolish things of the world to shame the wise; God chose the weak things of the world to shame the strong. God chose the lowly things of this world and the despised things—and the things that are not—to nullify the things that are."[32]

Sometimes the Lord chose slaves to teach the powerful of the earth. It is written:

"Now bands of raiders from Aram had gone out and had taken captive a young girl from Israel, and she served Naaman's wife. She said to her mistress, 'If only my master would see the prophet who is in Samaria! He would cure him of his leprosy.' Naaman went to the king and told him what the Israelite girl had said."[33]

Regarding this Ellen White comments:

"A slave, far from her home, this little maid was nevertheless one of God's witnesses, unconsciously fulfilling the purpose for which God had chosen Israel as His people. As she ministered in that heathen home, her sympathies were aroused in behalf of her master; and, remembering the wonderful miracles of healing wrought through Elisha, she said to her mistress, 'Would God my lord were with the prophet that is in Samaria! For he would recover him of his leprosy.' She knew that the power of Heaven was with Elisha, and she believed that by this power Naaman could be healed."[34]

A friend whom I consider high social stratum asked me, "Who do you consider to be the most influential person in the life of ...? citing a senior executive of the country."[35] I answered that I did not know, after a pause, he whispered it was his driver. No! After an inspiring conversation, I think he is not the most influential, but one of the most influential, which is not surprising judging by the influence of some servants in the Bible.[36] On this subject, Ellen White comments:

"Nehemiah, one of the Hebrew exiles, occupied a position of influence and honor in the Persian court. As cupbearer had free access to the royal presence ... Through this man ... God intended to bless His people in the land of their fathers."[37]

The power of the oikos

I believe in the power of the oikos. The scriptures teach, "Believe in the Lord Jesus, and you will be saved—you and your household" (Greek oikos).[38] Concerning the Gadarene ex-demoniac we read:

> "Jesus did not let him, but said, "Go home to your own people and tell them how much the Lord has done for you, and how he has had mercy on you."[39]

The Oikos: home, family home, can be intimate or extended.

In reference to the Shepherd of the lost and found sheep, we are told: "And when he finds it, he joyfully puts it on his shoulders and goes home. Then he calls his friends and neighbors together and says, 'Rejoice with me; I have found my lost sheep'"[40] The Oikos includes friends and neighbors plus colleagues and even bosses with whom we have a certain level of closeness.

Nehemiah was part of King Artaxerxes' oikos, the young slave was part of the oikos of arrogant Naaman, Daniel was part of Nebuchadnezzar oikos and Mordecai was part of Ahasuerus' one. Anyone could have a rich uncle to evangelize. In fact, the theory of six degrees of separation could give us an idea of the power of family networks (oikos) for evangelization.[41]

Undoubtedly special gifts are required for this special class, it is expected that the rich members of the church take the forefront of evangelization to the upper and middle class, but it is a myth to try to hold it exclusively to the them.

Among the reflections reported by Ellen White on working with the upper class are the following findings and principles:

1. The reality of neglect in the evangelization of the upper strata: "The higher classes have been strangely neglected"[42]

2. The mandate of inclusive evangelization: "The gospel is to harmonize the sinful race. It is to bring rich and poor together at the feet of Jesus."[43]

3. The quality of the workers God requires: "God calls for

earnest, humble workers, who will carry the gospel to the higher class."[44]

4. The reality of the spiritual gifts: "Some people are especially gifted to work for the higher classes."[45]

Communicating the Gospel in a manner that is consistent and dedicated:

"Many suppose that in order to reach the higher classes, a manner of life and method of work must be adopted that will be suited to their fastidious tastes… This is an error. The way of worldly policy is not God's way of reaching the higher classes. That which will reach them effectually is a consistent, unselfish presentation of the gospel of Christ."[46]

The need for appropriate methods:

"There is a certain round of labor performed in a certain way that leaves a large class untouched…"[47] "The intelligent, the refined, are altogether too much passed by. The hook is not baited to catch this class, and ways and methods are not prayerfully devised to reach them with truth that is able to make them wise unto salvation."[48]

The promise of success in evangelism to the upper strata:

"There are miracles to be wrought in genuine conversions, —miracles that are not now discerned. The greatest men of this earth are not beyond the power of a wonder-working God."[49]

Special groups

By special groups I mean those segments that require a particular approach. An exhaustive list could include the deaf, the blind, the disabled, ethnic minorities, the illiterate, prisoners, addicts, the sick, the social isolation, homosexuals, among others, who are also candidates for the eternal kingdom.

I know that at all levels of our congregation we should have some sort of response to this concern, but I mean something more convincing and impressive, something real and practical to reach the hearts and minds of members. This only seeks to encourage reflection. The third angel must reach those dozens of groups in our communities who are waiting for us.

Regarding the ministry of evangelization of the deaf, just to give an example, over the course of writing this book Arthur Griffith, who was ordained as the first minister for the deaf in the Adventist Church in 1969, died at age 89, and according to

Ansel Oliver who reports on Adventist News Network, in North America there are approximately 300 members of the Adventist Church divided into five congregations, but he notes that only 2-4 percent of the population of two million deaf people in the United States attends a church of any kind.

A fact that I find poignant is the nostalgic confession of Alfred, son of Griffin and pastor of two deaf communities in California, who said: "Deaf people are an isolated subculture" complaining that other denominations go before the Adventists in their evangelistic ministry to this community.[50]

13th Evangelistic Principle

Establish concrete plans to reach the middle, upper classes and special groups.

By the grace of God, great camels will pass through the eye of the needle.

PRACTICAL IDEAS

1. While you determine your own, help church members to establish their own oikos.

2. Prayerfully choose one or two wealthy persons of your oikos to take the gospel to them.

3. Identify some people from middle and upper strata in your community and begin to bring them some Adventist literature.

4. Offer help to a brother or sister of medium or high stratum of your church to form a small group.

5. Make a prayer list for the rich people.

6. Be sure to have an orderly and inspiring worship.

7. Make a detailed strategic plan for the church with ideas to achieve these classes.

Aim today by the grace of Christ to be an useful instrument in the hands of the great Master to evangelize special segments!

SECTION V

Success in Urban Evangelization

This section focuses on the need for our houses of worship to be perceived as real cities of refuge, shelters of love and peace, homes to an inspiring worship and social work with focus on fulfilling the mission! Some of the wonderful promises of God to fund his work are studied here and the Holy Spirit is highlighted as the missionary leader of the church by excellence.

Chapter 14

Cities of Refuge

O NE OF THE MOST distinctive symbols of hope that existed in
Israel was constituted by the cities of refuge, of which the
Bible states:

"Then the LORD said to Joshua:"Tell the Israelites to designate the
cities of refuge, as I instructed you through Moses, so that anyone
who kills a person accidentally and unintentionally may flee there
and find protection from the avenger of blood. When they flee to one
of these cities, they are to stand in the entrance of the city gate and
state their case before the elders of that city. Then the elders are to
admit the fugitive into their city and provide a place to live among
them."[1]

Although it was necessary to follow the rigorous legal
process and determine the veracity of the version the refugee
requested, it is obvious that these six cities represented a last
hope for the confused murderer.

Some features found in the Bible about the cities of refuge
and house rules are:

- They were part of God's promises to Israel concerning
  the promised land.[2]

- The roads should be clear, and the cities strategically
  located.[3]

- The first cities of refuge on this side of Jordan were set
  apart by Moses.[4] The SDA Bible Commentary highlights the fact that the word used in this text to divide,

is the same used Scripture in Deuteronomy 10:8, referring to the selection of the tribe of Levi to carry the
sacred furniture of the tabernacle.[5]

- They were strictly to house whom had killed his neighbor without meaning to, that is, without being unintentionally estranged.[6]

- They had the express intention of saving lives.[7]

- They were Levite cities[8]

- They served as refuge from the avenger of blood, both
Israelites and foreigners, until the trial was known.[9]

- The laws to prosecute these cases were very explicit.[10]

- When the innocent was absolved, his stay was confirmed in the city of refuge, that he should live, without leaving at any moment, until the death of the high
priest, or risk being killed by the avenger.[11]

- Rescuing those who fled to the city of refuge was not
allowed. He could not pay a fine to go home.[12]

- The fugitives were to be received immediately within
the city, where they received provisional accommoda-
tions until the day of judgment. Under no circumstances
could they be delivered to the processing avenger of
blood until his guilt at trial was found.[13]

- The declared culprit was out taken out of the city of
refuge and delivered to the avenger of blood by the
elders of his own city.[14]

Think of that poor man who unintentionally killed his
neighbor! By mistake!, (but now is also pursued by the avenger
of blood, the nearest relative of the deceased). Thanks to God the
city is less than half a day's journey and the road is in good condition and well marked, however he does not cease the crying
and remembering his friend and the confusion of the accident. He
remembers his wife with whom he lives a honeymoon, and who
two days ago had told him he was going to be a dad. What a pity!
But all is not lost; at least he can save his life, he will live among
holy people and keep watch to ensure the death of the high priest,
though without desiring it. - So I imagine it. -

Will he find exile in the real Refuge? What role will his new family play? Those who once fled or were called to minister to the wounded and wandering. The picture evoked by these texts bears a strong resemblance to the plan of salvation. The cities of refuge are a clear symbol of Christ and his church. The whole gospel can be presented through this principle.[15]

Ellen G. White says,

"The cities of refuge were so distributed as to be within a half day's journey of every part of the land. The roads leading to them were always to be kept in good repair; all along the way signposts were to be erected bearing the word "Refuge" in plain, bold characters, that the fleeing one might not be delayed for a moment. ... The cities of refuge appointed for God's ancient people were a symbol of the refuge provided in Christ. The same merciful Saviour who appointed those temporal cities of refuge has by the shedding of His own blood provided for the transgressors of God's law a sure retreat, into which they may flee for safety from the second death."[16]

Christ is our new city of refuge. He said, "Come to Me, all *you* who labor and are heavy laden, and I will give you rest."[17] The church is the house of prayer and therefore is the place to those who to Him.[18] "The church is God's fortress, His city of refuge, which He holds in a revolted world."[19] In light of this powerful statement I wonder, how aware are we of our mission? How relevant are we in our environment? Are our churches seen as symbols of hope? Would we be missed if we left the community? How well are we marked as heavenly shelters?

I will highlight five basic issues that undoubtedly would make us relevant in our environment:

1. Restore love as the first principle of evangelism

Jesus said, "By this all will know that you are My disciples, if you have love for one another."[20] So the first evangelistic principle is love.

As shelters of Christ we are a spiritual refuge and therefore the manifestation of genuine love is essential. The apostle Paul expresses this by saying:

"And though I have *the gift of* prophecy, and understand all mysteries and all knowledge, and though I have all faith, so that I could remove mountains, but have not love, I am nothing."[21]

One statement has impacted my pastoral life: "If we would humble ourselves before God, and be kind and courteous and tenderhearted and pitiful, there would be one hundred conversions to the truth where now there is only one."[22] Courteous, tenderhearted and pitiful, who would say that we can centuple the results? I think we should reflect and ask how well are we connected with our neighbors? How well do we moderate the volume of our sound equipment? This also is evangelism.

2. Revive the primitive unit as an evangelizing principle

The unit is a powerful evangelism principle and Jesus in his well known intercessory prayer in John 17 He pleaded:

> "I do not pray for these alone, but also for those who will believe in Me through their word; that they all may be one, as You, Father, are in Me, and I in You; that they also may be one in Us, that the world may believe that You sent Me."[23]

Words inspire, but example move. The world will believe not so much what we say but what we live. No wonder Ellen White said vehemently:

> "If Christians were to act in concert, moving forward as one, under the direction of one Power, for the accomplishment of one purpose, they would move the world."[24]

A divided church cannot fulfill its mission. Unity is vital. It was not coincidentally that the disciples were unanimous in prayer in the upper room before being invested with the heavy early rain.

Ellen G. White emphasizes this principle in the two following statements:

> "Harmony and union existing among men of varied dispositions is the strongest witness that can be borne that God has sent His Son into the world to save sinners."[25]

> "The golden chain of love, binding the hearts of the believers in unity, in bonds of fellowship and love, and in oneness with Christ and the Father, makes the connection perfect, and bears to the world a testimony of the power of Christianity that cannot be controverted."[26]

This unity is the natural result of love and it will lead people to the empathic mind of Christ Jesus. The testimony the early church has given us is abundant, "had all things in common", "none claimed to be theirs nothing that had", "no needy between them."[27] More than that, this feeling is registered in the entire Bible as a witness of faith of the true religion throughout the ages. For whatever things were written before were written for our learning[28] I invite you to reflect on the following texts:

> "Is this not the fast that I have chosen: To loose the bonds of wickedness, To undo the heavy burdens, To let the oppressed go free, and that you break every yoke? *Is it* not to share your bread with the hungry, and that you bring to your house the poor who are cast out; when you see the naked, that you cover him, and not hide yourself from your own flesh? Then your light shall break forth like the morning, your healing shall spring forth speedily, and your righteousness shall go before you; the glory of the Lord shall be your rear guard."[29]

> "Pure and undefiled religion before God and the Father is this: to visit orphans and widows in their trouble, and to keep oneself unspotted from the world."[30]

Remember:

> "Men may combat and defy our logic, they may resist our appeals; but a life of disinterested love is an argument they cannot gainsay. A consistent life, characterized by the meekness of Christ, is a power in the world."[31]

Although it seems incredible, to meet the 'real' needs of God's people inside of our local churches is a solid and anchored biblical principle of urban evangelism in the Word of God.

3. Revise the dynamics of our worship services

It is presumed that a shelter has specific qualities and is equipped as such. A person who turns on the TV to watch sports is not expecting to see the news. In the same way, as churches we must be crystal clear that people who come are looking for comfort, hope, love, guidance and comprehension, must meet a service that will supply those needs.

Ellen G. White wrote:

> "To the humble, believing soul, the house of God on earth is the gate of heaven. The song of praise, the prayer, the words spoken by Christ's representatives, are God's appointed agencies to prepare a people for the church above, for that loftier worship into which there can enter nothing that defileth."[32]

The worship service is an encounter between the sinner and the God Almighty and the vehicle are the songs of praise, prayer and the preaching of the Word. A few days ago I spoke with a college professor who visits several of our churches and mentioned one in particular. About that one she confessed that stopped attending because they spent too much time giving announcements and she was interested in the message.

Christian A. Schwarz in his book Natural Church Development presents an inspiring worship as one of the eight basic characteristics of a healthy church. The truth is that "when worship is inspiring, it draws people to the services 'all by itself.' "[33]

I visualize an inspiring worship focused on God as the sole subject of all worship. The anthropocentric worships are anti-biblical. It should be understandable and engaging for worshipers, but that develops with order. Punctuality is vital. I remember what one of my teachers always said, "Punctuality is a courtesy of kings, a duty of knights and a virtue of holy people." It is convenient to define at what time worship starts and ends and respect that time. Our Sabbath worship usually takes three to three and a half hours, that's enough time if everything is done decently and in order.[34]

SERVICE TIME EXECUTION

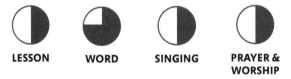

LESSON   WORD   SINGING   PRAYER &
                                    WORSHIP

If we dedicate at least 30 minutes for the study of the lesson, 45 minutes for the preaching of the Word, 30 minutes of congregational singing and special musical performances and 30 minutes of prayer and worship, through the presentation of God's tithes and offerings, it still leaves us at least 45 minutes for all other ornaments and to be punctual in starting and ending.

Our services can be one of the major evangelistic tools of the church when well oriented. When misguided, they are a threat to accomplishing the mission because a first comer does not feel inspired to return.

4. Revalue our social responsibility

Dr. Pedrito U. Maynard-Reid, in his book Complete Evangelism, reviews how since 1900 the idea has grown that evangelism and social action are incompatible, which he judged to be unbiblical, because it concentrates on proving untruth to raise that true evangelism includes the personal, spiritual and social dimension being a vertical relationship with God and horizontal relationship with other people in the society.[35]

His approach reminds us of Christ's method outlined by Ellen White when she says:

"Christ's method alone will give true success in reaching the people. The Saviour mingled with men as one who desired their good. He showed His sympathy for them, ministered to their needs, and won their confidence. Then He bade them, 'Follow Me.'"[36]

The Savior met the needs of the people! This is perfectly consistent with the issues raised by Scripture. Matthew reports:

"And when Jesus went out He saw a great multitude; and He was moved with compassion for them, and healed their sick. When it was evening, His disciples came to Him, saying, 'This is a deserted place, and the hour is already late. Send the multitudes away, that they may go into the villages and buy themselves food.' But Jesus said to them, 'They do not need to go away. You give them something to eat.'"[37]

How contrasting was the attitude of the disciples of Christ! They seemed to be interested but did not want to get involved. Who told the disciples that these people had no money to buy food? They simply assumed. It is easy to send people home with lots of biblical verses and an emotional 'God bless you'. In the meantime the Lord admonishes us, "There is no need to go away, give them something to eat."

The early church did not neglect the preaching, but also cared about the widows tables.[38]

"It is only by an unselfish interest in those in need of help that we can give a practical demonstration of the truths of the gospel."[39]

How to help? What is the basis to establish our social theology? First, **"unity is strength"**; the early church cooperated each one according to his strength.[40] Second, I think that although the relevance we seek is indivisible in its strong social implications, its ultimate goal is spiritual. According to the following story there is a beautiful principle to learn.

> "Now Peter and John went up together to the temple at the hour of prayer, the ninth *hour*. And a certain man lame from his mother's womb was carried, whom they laid daily at the gate of the temple which is called Beautiful, to ask alms from those who entered the temple; who, seeing Peter and John about to go into the temple, asked for alms. And fixing his eyes on him, with John, Peter said, 'Look at us.' So he gave them his attention, expecting to receive something from them. Then Peter said, 'Silver and gold I do not have, but what I do have I give you: In the name of Jesus Christ of Nazareth, rise up and walk.'"[41]

The church often lacks material resources as in the times of Peter and John, but they were equipped with powerful spiritual resources that wisely managed become a powerful medicine of material kind. What has the Seventh-day Adventist Church to give?

Undoubtedly the list is headed by health topics, nutrition and healthy food, but you can add family counseling, education, family finances and many more that could be listed.

God has given this authority to His Church on the health subject, which has been recognized by institutions such as National Geographic, in its Magazine on November 2005 with the report about the secrets of a long life.[42] It is also important to note the collaboration agreement between the Seventh-day Adventist Church and the Pan American Health Organization on July 26, 2011. That is what Ellen White called health reform, the entering wedge, the right arm or as a psychologist friend of my family suggested, the skillful hand. In any case the intention is to open the door to the gospel message, a kind of helpmate for evangelization! Some of the statements of the prophet of the Lord concerning all things to be done in the field of health are:

- "Health reform, wisely treated, will prove an entering wedge where the truth may follow with marked success."[43]

- "The opening of hygienic restaurants is a work that God would have done in the cities. If wisely conducted, these restaurants will be missionary centers. Those working in them should have at hand publications on health and temperance topics and on other phases of gospel truth, to give to those coming for meals."[44]

- "Cooking schools are to be held. The people are to be taught how to prepare wholesome food. They are to be shown the need of discarding unhealthful foods. But we should never advocate a starvation diet. It is possible to have a wholesome, nutritious diet without the use of tea, coffee, and flesh food. The work of teaching the people how to prepare a dietary that is at once wholesome and appetizing, is of the utmost importance."[45]

- Why do we establish sanitariums? That the sick who come to them for treatment may receive relief from physical suffering and may also receive spiritual help."[46]

- "Our sanitariums are the right hand of the gospel, opening ways whereby suffering humanity may be reached with the glad tidings of healing through Christ."[47]

- "Education in health principles was never more needed than now... Many transgress the laws of health through ignorance, and they need instruction..."[48]

Although the work of health is an open door to the gospel which is self evident in the ministry of Christ, education in family matters, including financial management, it is undoubtedly another great opportunity to present truth.

The issue of finance is vibrant in all the Scriptures, according to Larry Burkett, co-founder of Crown Financial Ministries, the Bible contains 2,350 verses dealing with money and how to handle possessions.[49] Regarding the same, Edward Reed, editor of Faith and Finance says, "Two thirds of the parables of Jesus are related to money and material possessions."[50] An argument that points to over two thousand biblical references dealing with this topic, compared to about five hundred verses about prayer and less than five hundred exposing the issue of faith.

In reality, this emphasis of Scripture is more than justified since money is the main competitor for the lordship of Christ in the heart. Jesus expressed this by saying:

> "No man can serve two masters, for either he will hate the one and love the other, or be loyal to one and despise the other. You cannot serve God and money.[51]

Money is not evil[52] but the "love of money is the root of all evil." Millions of families in bankruptcy, material and spiritual paralytic, cry out for help to a church that has no gold or silver, but undoubtedly has a lot to give. The same applies to issues such as marriage, family values and education, among others.

5. Consider giving more and better utilizing the buildings of worship

Although this goal may be closely related to the above I prefer to treat separately. While it is true that once our community outreach approach is invigorated together with the spiritual, our houses of worship will have more and better use, the fact remains that God's house is still a house meeting between the sinner and God, a house of offerings and a house of prayer.[53]

Acquiring a property of 500 square meters for a church with facilities for two hundred people could be found in the center of Santo Domingo, being conservative, for RD $20,000,000.00 (U.S.$500,000.00). An adequate building for such a property would cost no less than RD$30,000,000.00 (U.S. $750,000.00), for a total of RD$50,000,000.00 (U.S. $1,250,000.00). Imagine that in that place instead of building a church we could build two! Yes, I mean two parallel congregations, but completely separated from each other, one on the first level and the other on the third one; the second level would be left to share offices and children's classroom. This has been tested with great success!

RD$ 20MM ($500,000)   FOR SALE   RD$ 30MM ($750,000)

RD$ 50MM ($1.25 MM)

How about if each of these two congregations decided by the grace of God, to also advance to two services, we could reach a thousand people gathering every Saturday in a building that was originally designed for 500. It is a matter of policy, planning and understanding that "the structure is at the service of the mission, not the mission at the service of the structure."

I've heard of churches in Haiti that before the earthquake were offering three services per Sabbath and I know that congregations such as the Jehovah's Witnesses, gather several congregations on different days of the week in the same Kingdom Hall.

The idea is not to create condo churches, much less concentrate forces. Ellen G. White herself warned:

> "As a people we have been in danger of centering too many important interests in one place. This is not good judgment or wisdom. An interest is now to be created in the principal cities. Many small centers must be established, rather than a few large centers..."[54]

The idea is that the churches are able to identify somewhere in your own building or even environment in which to develop new congregations after mature a little can be transplanted to other places or stay in the same place if the conditions are provided. I think that we have nothing to lose and everything to gain. Let's try new methods!

14ᵗʰ Evangelistic Principle

Pray and work.

Until we convert our churches into true shelters, and centers of hope and teaching for a world that is perishing for a lack of knowledge. Although this is also a challenge, I dream it as the success of urban evangelism.

PRACTICAL IDEAS

1. Decide as a church to prioritize attention to the needy in the local congregation.

2. Identify a basic need of your community and study solid plans to supply it.

3. Evaluate your worship service on such specifics as the preaching of the Word, music, punctuality, active participation of the worshipers, worship in tithes and offerings and plan how to improve it.

4. If your church is more than eighty percent full, it is full, think about new ideas to grow and move with urgency.

5. Offer your community vegetarian cooking courses, biblical finances and family education.

Aims today by the grace of Christ to assist your church to become a true city of refuge!

Chapter 15

Not by Power, but by My Spirit

THIS CHAPTER TAKES ITS NAME from the words of the prophet Zechariah to Zerubbabel, first governor of Judah after the exile. Be amazed by this beautiful statement:

"Then he answered and spoke unto me, saying, This is the word of the LORD to Zerubbabel: Not by power, but by my Spirit, saith the Lord of hosts."[1]

Zerubbabel probably came to Jerusalem in the summer of 536 BC, and immediately began preparations for the rebuilding of the temple, coming to lay the foundation in the following spring, but their enemies could not stop the work until the second year of Darius (520 - 519 BC).[2]

The Seventh-day Adventist Bible Commentary details that Zerubbabel and his friends were depressed for their lack of capacity and resources to continue the work of restoration as they faced their enemies. Revelation presented that success would be achieved by the Spirit of God and not by human strength.[3]

Likewise the great work of evangelizing the cities will not be achieved by human forces, but by the power of God. The Holy Spirit is willing to make greater than the miracles of Pentecost. The Supreme Lord is the Administrator of his church and as evidence I refer six actions of ecclesiastical attributed to God, and some of them directly to the person of the Holy Spirit:

1. God is the one who teaches: "When the Spirit of truth comes, he will guide you into all truth: for he will not

speak on his own authority, but will speak whatever he hears, and he will show you things to come. "[4]

2. God is the one who adds: "... And the Lord added to the church daily those who were being saved."[5]

3. God is the giver of the gifts, "And He Himself gave some to be apostles, some prophets, some to be evangelists, and some pastors and teachers, for the equipping of the saints for the work of ministry, for building up the body of Christ."[6]

4. God is the one who sends: "And the Spirit said to Philip, Go near, and join thyself to this chariot. Philip ran up and heard him reading Isaiah the prophet and said, 'Do you understand what you read?'"[7]

5. God the one who calls: "As they ministered to the Lord and fasting, the Holy Spirit said. Separate Barnabas and Saul for the work to which I have called."[8]

6. It is God who makes it grow: "I planted, Apollo watered it, but God made it grow."[9]

Facing such a refreshing reality, we have no reason to fear! However, although the Holy Spirit is the great administrator of his Church, the man has an important job to do. Zerubbabel did not interpret the message of the prophet Zechariah as an invitation to neglect their responsibilities, he knew very well that God will never do for his people which has given them the ability to do for themselves. Although the victory would come from God, they would not discard the sword or the army, it was rather a call to trust and work, without being distressed.

It is true that in 2011 we had one Adventist for every 3,250 Chinese, i.e. 400 thousand Adventists against 1.3 billion citizens, but is there anything impossible for God? Ron E. M. Clouzet is right to argue that the outpouring of the Holy Spirit is the greatest need of Adventism.[10] "The secret of success lies in the union of divine power with human effort."[11]

Money and consecration

To the question about how to finance this great work of evangelization, I answer: It's part of the great miracles the Holy Spirit has reserved for the last days, but since there are always conditions that the people of God must fulfill. In that regard Ellen White wrote:

> "In the last extremity, before this work shall close, thousands will be cheerfully laid upon the altar. Men and women will feel it a blessed privilege to share in the work of preparing souls to stand in the great day of God, and they will give hundreds as readily as dollars are given now."[12]

Any veteran Adventist knows that one of the statements that has caught the attention of the Seventh-day Adventist Church, of those outlined by Ellen White is: "God's people are called to a work that requires money and consecration. The obligations resting upon us hold us responsible to work for God to the utmost of our ability."[13]

For many, the surprise is not the combination of concepts, but money comes first. Personally, I do not think the concepts are necessarily in order of importance, she is just saying that in order to expedite the work of evangelization it is needed in addition to abundant economic resources, a holy people, or if you will, in addition to a holy people, abundant economic resources.

Fortunately God is the true owner of everything that exists, we are mere stewards of His property.

> "Jehovah is the earth and its fullness, the world and those who dwell therein. For he founded it upon the seas and established it upon the rivers."[14]

Both consecration and money are gifts of the Spirit that God will give abundantly to His Church to fulfill its great task of evangelizing the cities, but these resources will not only come from the people of God, Ellen G. White also wrote:

> "I am greatly encouraged to believe that many persons not of our faith will help considerably by their means. The light given me is that in many places, especially in the great cities of America, help will be given by such persons."[15]

Obviously as it happened in the Red Sea it is necessary to march first. If the church believes and works, will see the glory of God.

> "I have had messages from the Lord, which I have given to our people over and over again, that there are many monied men who are susceptible to the influences and impressions of the gospel message... God will move upon the hearts of monied men, when the

Bible, and the Bible alone, is presented as the light of the world. In these cities the truth is to go forth as a lamp that burneth." [16]

Those who work in the large cities are to reach if possible to the high ones of the world, even to ruling powers. Where is our faith? God has presented to me the case of Nebuchadnezzar. The Lord worked with power to bring the mightiest king on the earth to acknowledge Him as King over all kings. [17]

To evangelize the cities, God requires new wineskins, the world drunk with the wine of Babylon should taste the new wine of God. [18] Only the Holy Spirit can convert the old wineskin of your life in a new one for the Lord!" [19] Before becoming witnesses we must receive power. Jesus said. "... You will receive power when there come upon you the Holy Spirit, and you will be my witnesses in Jerusalem, throughout Judea, in Samaria, and unto the uttermost part of the earth." [20]

Let it be our prayer as we move to the Upper Room:

Hover o'er me, Holy Spirit,
Bathe my trembling heart and brow;
Fill me with Thy hallowed presence,
Come, O come and fill me now.

Refrain
Fill me now, fill me now,
Jesus, come and fill me now.
Fill me with Thy hallowed presence,
Come, O come and fill me now.

Thou canst fill me, gracious Spirit,
Though I cannot tell Thee how;
But I need Thee, greatly need Thee;
Come, O come and fill me now.

I am weakness, full of weakness;
At Thy sacred feet I bow;
Blest, divine, eternal Spirit,
Fill with love, and fill me now.

Cleanse and comfort, bless and save me;
Bathe, O, bathe my heart and brow;
Thou art comforting and saving,
Thou art sweetly filling now. [21]

15ᵗʰ Evangelistic Principle

Recognize it is not by our own strength.

although we should strive to reach the cities, it is ultimately a task that will be accomplished not by our own strength or wisdom, but by the Spirit of God.

PRACTICAL IDEAS

7. Enter daily into your upper room and read at least one chapter of the Bible.

8. Plan with your church the reading of the books: Last Day Events and The Great Controversy, of Ellen White

9. Form prayer groups asking for the Holy Spirit.

Aim today by the grace of Christ, to be a new wineskin, filled with the power of the Holy Spirit!

References

Introduction

1. Pep Vivas i Elias et ali., Ventanas en la ciudad: Observaciones sobre las urbes contemporáneas (Barcelona, Editorial UOC, 2005), p. 69

2. Horacio Capel, La definición de lo urbano. Estudios Geográficos, nº 138-139 (nº especial de "Homenaje al Profesor Manuel de Terán"), febrero-mayo 1975, p 265-301

3. American Journal of Sociology

4. José Ortega y Gasset. La rebelión de las masas (Madrid, Espasa – Calpe/Colección Austral, 1995), p. 12

5. Antonio Cruz, El Cristianismo en la aldea global (Florida: Vida, 2003), p. 30

6. John 4:35

7. Oscar Andrés, Cardenal Rodríguez, Desafíos de la Misión en la Posmodernidad, en http://www.elsalvadormisionero.org/node/186 (Accesado e l 28-12-12)

8. Francisco Niño, La Iglesia en la Ciudad: El Fenómeno de las grandes ciudades en América Latina como problema teológico y como desafío pastoral (Italia, Iura Editionis et versionis reservantur, 1996)

9. Colegio teológico evangélico internacional y seminario Anglicano establecido en la Universidad de Oxford

10. Michael Green & Alister McGrath, ¿Cómo llegar a ellos? (Barcelona: Clie, 2003), p.16

11. Barry A. Kosmin and Ariela Keysar, American Religion Identification Survey 2008. Summary Report (Hartford: Trinity College, March 2009).

12. Jon Paulien, Everlasting Gospel, Ever - Changing World (Idaho: Pacific Press Publishing Association, 2008), p. 10

13. Proverbs 22:3

14. See Ted N. C. Wilson, A las Puertas. Un llamado al Reavivamiento y la Reforma (Florida: APIA/ México: GEMA, 2008), pp. 101 - 118

15. John Dybdahl, Adventist Mission in 21th Century (Hagerstown: Review and Herald Publishing Association, 1999), p. 17 - 18

Section I
The Metropolitan Context

Chapter 1 - A Look at the Cities

1. United Nations, World Urbanization Prospects: The 2010 Revision, in http://esa.un.org/wpp/Other-Information/faq.htm#q1(Accessed on February 25, 2012)

2. Matthew 24:14

3. United Nations, World Urbanization Prospects: The 2009 Revision. Highlights p. 3

4. Samuel González Jirón. Introducción al Urbanismo p. 1, in http://es.scribd.com/doc/52985899/Urbanismo (Accessed on May 10, 2012)

5. Horacio Capel, La definición de lo urbano: Estudios Geográficos, nº 138-139, febrero-mayo 1975, p 265-301

6. Thierry Dutour, La ciudad medieval: orígenes y triunfo de la Europa Urbana (Barcelona: Paidós, 2004), p.29

7. United Nations, Population Division 9, World Urbanization Prospects: The 2009 Revision, p. 14

8. Ibid p. 126

9. Andrew Davey, Cristianismo Urbano y Globalización (London, Editorial SAL TER-RAE, 2001), p. 24

10. United Nations, Population Division 9, World Urbanization Prospects: The 2014 Revision, p. 14

11. IDEM

12. United Nations, Population Division 9, World Urbanization Prospects: The 2014 Revision, p. 1

13. UN – HABITAT. Urbanización: Mega y metaciudades, ¿las nuevas ciudades-estados? in http//www.unhabitat.org. (Accessed on February 25, 2012)

14. Rudi Maier, Encountering God in Life and Mission: The Urban Church in Postmodern World, By Kleber De Oliveira Goncalves. (Berrien Spring Michigan: Department of World Mission Andrews University Press, 2010), p. 269

15. Genesis 11: 1-8

16. Samuel González Jirón. Introducción al Urbanismo p. 98, in http://es.scribd.com/doc/52985899/Urbanismo (Accesed on May 10, 2012)

17. Jesús Leal Maldonado. La Ciudad y lo Urbano, in http://www.ucm.es/info/eurotheo/diccionario/C/ciudad_urbano.pdf (Accessed on December 20, 2012)

18. En Horacio Capel, La definición de lo urbano. Estudios Geográficos, nº 138-139 (nº especial de "Homenaje al Profesor Manuel de Terán"), febrero-mayo 1975, p 265-301

19. Ellen Gould White, "The Adventist Home", 1952, p. 135.2.

20. Ellen Gould White, "The Adventist Home", 1952, p. 135.1.

21. UN – HABITAT. Urbanización: Mega y metaciudades, ¿las nuevas ciudades-estados? Web: www.unhabitat.org., (Accessed on February 25, 2012) op cit.

22. Metrópolis 2011, Autoridad del Espacio Público de la Ciudad de México: Megaciudades, Informe de la Comisión 4, p. 5

23. Galatians 4:4

24. Ellen Gould White, "The Upward Look", 1982, p. 362.2.

25. Ellen Gould White, "El ministerio médico (Idaho: Pacific Press, 2003) p. 403

26. Exodus 14:15; Joshua 4:23

Chapter 2 - A Look at the Citizens

1. John Dybdahl, Adventist Mission in 21th Century (Hagerstown: Review and Herald Publishing Association,1999), p. 63

2. Kleber De Oliveira, Misión urbana en un mundo posmodernista, not puslished study.

3. Jon Paulien, Everlasting Gospel, Ever - Changing World (Idaho: Pacific Press Publishing Association, 2008), p. 27

4. See 1 Corinthians 2:14

5. See 2 Timothy 3:1 - 7

6. See Matthew 24:37 - 39

7. Joao Batista Libanio, La Iglesia en la Ciudad., p. 118, en www.seleccionesdeteologia.net/selecciones/llib/vol37/146/146 (Accessed on March 15, 2012)

8. See John 1:29

9. John Dybdahl, Adventist Mission in 21th Century (Hagerstown: Review and Herald Publishing Association,1999), p. 65

10. Jon Paulien, Everlasting Gospel, Ever - Changing World (Idaho: Pacific Press Publishing Association, 2008), pp. 28 - 32

11. For a deeper study in the subject of meta-related read, Richard Bauckham, Bible and Mission. Christian Witness in a postmodern World (Carlisle: Paternoster Press/Grand

Rapids, Baker Book House, 2003), pp 85 -94

12. See Hermes Tavera, 2012 y el verdadero fin del mundo (Idaho: Pacific Press, 2011)

13. Michael Green & Alister McGrath, ¿Cómo llegar a ellos? (Barcelona: Clie, 2003), p.37

14. Ernan A. Norman, A strategy for reaching secular people. The intentional church in a post – modern World (Bloomington: Autor House, 2007), pp. 133, 134

15. Ibid, pp., 136 - 137

16. Ibid, p. 157

17. Ibid, pp. 177 - 238

18. Michael Green & Alister McGrath, ¿Cómo llegar a ellos? (Barcelona: Clie, 2003), p. 52

19. See John 13:34

20. See Leviticus 19:18

21. Ellen Gould White, "The Ministry of Healing", 1905, p. 143.3

22. Joao Batista Libanio, La Iglesia en la Ciudad, en www.seleccionesdeteologia.net/selecciones/llib/vol37/146/146 (Accessed on March 15, 2012)

23. Ellen Gould White, "Education", 1903, p. 78.3

24. Ellen Gould White, "Testimonies for the Church Volume 9", 1909, p. 28.4

Section II
The Urban Mission

Chapter 3 - The Mission of the Prophet

1. Amos 7:14

2. 2 Kings 22:14 - 20

3. León J. Wood, Los Profetas de Israel (Grand Rapids: Editorial Portavoz, 2012), p. 13

4. 1 Samuel 9:6 – 7:20; 2 Kings 14:1- 16; 2 Kings 5:20 -27; John 4:19

5. José L. Sicre, Los profetas de Israel y su Mensaje (Sevilla: Ediciones Cristiandad, 1986), p. 19

6. George E. Rice, Teología Fundamentos de Nuestra Fe. Los dones espirituales (Florida: APIA/ México: GEMA, 2005), p. 115

7. Abraham J. Herschel, Los Profetas. El hombre y su vocación (Buenos Aires: Editorial Paidós, s. d.), p. 29

8. Ibid, p. 36

9. Amos 3:7

10. Genesis 18: 16 - 33

11. Gary V. Smith, Los profetas como predicadores (Nashville, B& H Publishing Group, 2012), p. 6

12. Jude 14

13. Abraham J. Herschel, Los Profetas. El hombre y su vocación. (Buenos Aires: Editorial Paidós, s. d.), p. 20

14. Jeremiah 20:8,9

15. 1 Corinthians 9:16

16. Exodus 4:1

17. Exodus 4:10

18. Exodus 4: 11, 12

19. Deuteronomy 34: 10 - 12

20. Matthew 12:31- 46

21. Luke 24:19

22. 2 Chronicles 36: 15, 16

23. Luke 13:34

24. IDEM

25. Matthew 28:20

26. 1 Peter 2:9

27. Richard Bauckham, Bible and Mission. Christian Witness in a postmodern World (Carlisle: Paternoster Press/Grand Rapids, Baker Book House, 2003), pp 27 - 45

28. Genesis 12: 1- 3

29. Exodus 19: 4 - 6

30. 1 Corinthians 1: 25 - 29

31. 1 Peter 3:15

32. Centrípeta: Las naciones vendrían a Israel; centrifuga: La iglesia iría a las naciones.

33. Comentario bíblico adventista del séptimo día (Idaho: Pacific Press, 1990) t. 7, p. 588

34. Ellen Gould White, "The Acts of the Apostles", 1911, p. 9.1.

35. Michael Grenn, la Iglesia Local Agente de Evangelización (Grand Rapids, Nueva Creación: 1996), pp. 159 - 163

Chapter 4 - A Prophetic People

1. Matthew 3:2; Mark 1:14; Matthew 6:33; Matthew 10:7; Matthew 12:28; Matthew 13:11; Luke 10:9, 11; Acts 1:3; Acts 8:12; Acts 19:8; Acts 20:25; Acts 28:23,31

2. Luke 17:20, 21

3. Luke 22:17,18

4. Matthew 25:31

5. Luke 17:20

6. Luke 17:24

7. 1 Thessalonians 4:16

8. Ellen Gould White, "The Great Controversy 1888", 1888, p. 347.2.

9. John 19:30

10. Acts 1:3

11. Ellen Gould White, "The Desire of Ages", 1898, pp. 829-835

12. Acts 2:17- 21

13. Acts 2: 18 - 28

14. Acts 2: 29 -36

15. Acts 2:34 -35

16. Acts 2:32 - 36

17. Both here and in Revelation 21:1, the greek verb *ginomai* among other definitions means: to be made, finished.

18. Exodus 40:35; 1 Kings 8:11

19. Ellen Gould White, "Testimony Treasures Volume 2", 1949, p. 67.2

20. Ellen Gould White, "Early Writings", 1882, p. 280.2.

21. Revelation 21:6

22. Joshua Caleb, The return of Elijah, John the Baptist and Jesus the Jewish and Christian Christ (EEUU, Paul S.Durgin, 2006), p. 2

23. Matthew 3:1-3

24. Isaiah 40

25. Luke 3:5-6

26. Malachi 3:1

27. Daniel 7:13

28. Ellen Gould White, "The Great Controversy", 1911, p. 424.2.

29. John 1:21

30. Matthew 17: 10 -12

31. Morris, L. Venden, The return of Elijah (Mountain View, California: Pacific Press, 1982), p. 31

32. Malachi 4:5,6

33. John 1:29

34. Isaiah 25:9

35. Elena G. de White, Consejos sobre el régimen alimenticio (Miami, Florida: APIA, s. d.), p. 98

36. Ellen Gould White, "The Desire of Ages", 1898, p. 101.2.

37. Morris, L. Venden, The return of Elijah (Mountain View, California: Pacific Press, 1982), pp. 35 – 36 around the possible application to Mrs. White.

38. Revelation 14:12; Revelation 19:10

39. Revelation 10:11

40. Morris, L. Venden, The return of Elijah (Mountain View, California: Pacific Press, 1982), p. 34

41. See 1 Kings 17:15-16

42. 1 Kings 18:18

43. Morris, L. Venden, The return of Elijah (Mountain View, California: Pacific Press, 1982), p. 37

44. Jonah 3:4

45. Elena G. de White, La evangelización de las ciudades (Florida: APIA/ México: GEMA, 2005), p. 13

46. Acts 17:23

47. 1 Corinthians 2:1, 2

48. George R. Knight, Nuestra organización ¿Aliada o Enemiga de la Gran Comisión? (Florida: APIA/ México: GEMA, 2007), p. 62

49. Norman Gulley ¡Cristo Viene! Un enfoque Cristocéntrico de los eventos de los últimos días (Buenos Aires: ACES, 2003), p.556

50. Ted N. C. Wilson, Almost Home, pp. 122

51. Elena G. de White, Consejos sobre el régimen alimenticio (Miami, Florida: APIA, s. d.), p. 89

52. Titus 2:13

Chapter 5 - Three Angels, One Gospel

1. Revelation 14:6

2. Revelation 14:14

3. Ellen Gould White, "Counsels on Diet and Foods", 1938, p. 76.2.

4. 2 Samuel 3:14

5. Haggai 1:13

6. Matthew 11:7, 10

7. Revelation 2:1

8. Hebrews 1:14

9. 2 Corinthians 4:7

10. 2 Corintians 5:17-20

11. Romans 1:1; Romans 15:19; Acts 20:24; 2 Corinthians 4:4

12. Galatians 1:8

13. Revelation 14: 6-8

14. Clifford Goldstein, Ataque contra el Lugar Santísimo (Florida: APIA/ México: GEMA, 2005), p. 82

15. Frank B Holbrook, Simposio sobre Daniel (Florida: APIA/ México: GEMA, 2008), p. 169 - 222

16. C. Mervyn Maxwell, Dios revela el futuro (Florida: APIA, 1989) 2da Edic., p. 250

17. Jacques B. Doukhan, Secretos de Apocalipsis (Florida: APIA/ México: GEMA, 2008), p. 126

18. C. Mervyn Maxwell, El destino del planeta en rebelión (Miami, Florida: APIA, 1993) 2da Edic., pp. 349 -364

19. See relation between judgement and gospel in Clifford Goldstein, Como fuego en mis huesos (Buenos Aires: ACES, 2001), pp. 35-54

20. Revelation 14:7, 9

21. Ellen Gould White, "Last Day Events", 1992, p. 202.2.

22. IDEM

23. Luke 4: 18,19

24. Luke 4:21

25. 1 Corinthians 15: 1 - 4

26. Isaiah 61:2

27. Matthew 28: 20

28. Ellen Gould White, "Last Day Events", 1992, p. 199.4.

29. Hans k. LA Rondelle, Las Profecías del fin (Buenos Aires: ACES, 1999), p. 367

Section III
The enemies of urban evangelization

Chapter 6 - The Church in Days of Noah

1. Matthew 24:38-39

2. Luke 17: 28,29

3. José Luis González y Luis Ángel López, Sentirte bien está en tus manos (Cantabria, Sal Terrae, 1999) P. 242

4. Jim George, La influencia de un hombre de Dios (Michigan: Editorial Porta Voz, 2003), p. 42

5. Ellen Gould White, "Reflecting Christ", 1985, p. 241.3.

6. Ellen Gould White, "Christian Service", 1925, p. 88.3.

7. Acts 1:8

8. Acts 4:31

9. 2 Peter 2:5

10. Ellen Gould White, "Reflecting Christ", 1985, p. 322.4.

11. Ezekiel 3: 8,9

12. John 20:19 -22

13. Nick Schifrin (16 de abril de 2012) Abc News, UK Police Help Recover Blind Woman's Novel, en http://abcnews.go.com/International/london police-recover-blind-womans/story?id=16149861 (Accessed on September 15, 2012)

14. Matthew 5:13

15. Matthew 5:16

16. Ephesians 3:10

17. Rudi Maier, Encountering God in Life and Mission: The Urban Church in Postmodern World. (Berrien Spring Michigan: Department of World Mission Andrews University Press, 2010) P. 273

18. See Mark 3:13, 14

19. Ellen Gould White, "Gospel Workers 1915", 1915, p. 138.6.

20. Ellen Gould White, "Christ's Object Lessons", 1900, p. 414.1.

21. Ellen Gould White, "The Desire of Ages", 1898, p. 195.2.

22. José María Iribarren, El porqué de los dichos. (Ediciones Aguilar: Madrid, 1974) 4ta. Edic., p. 402

Chapter 7 - Giants in Canaan

1. Numbers 13: 28

2. Numbers 13:31-33

3. Deuteronomy 9:2

4. 1 Samuel 17:4

5. Cited by Luis Salvador Carulla and Marco Garrido Cumbrera, Prejuicio social y discapacidad (Madrid: UPC, 2005), p. 178

6. Ibid, p. 173

7. Ibid, p. 172

8. Dennis Coon, Fundamentos de Psicología (México, D. F.: Thomson, 2005) 10 Edic., p. 517, 518

9. Luke 6:37

10. Dennis Coon, Fundamentos de Psicología (México, D. F.: Thomson, 2005) 10 Edic., p. 517, 518

11. Luke 7:24

12. Numbers 13:31-33

13. Humberto Galimberti, Diccionario de Psicología (Madrid: Siglo XXI, 2002), p. 210

14. Mark 2: 15- 17

15. Ellen Gould White, "This Day With God", 1979, p. 269.5.

16. Ephesians 2:13,14

17. Romans 1:16

18. 1 Corinthians 1:18, 23-24

19. John 1:46

20. Daniel 1:12,13

21. Carmelo Monedero Gil, Psicopatología humana, (Madrid: Siglo XXI de España Editores, S.A.,1996), p. 420

22. Numbers 14:1

23. Ellen Gould White, "The Story of Redemption", 1947, p. 158.3.

24. Numbers 14:9

25. Joshua 15:14

26. Norman Gulley ¡Cristo Viene! Un enfoque Cristocéntrico de los eventos de los últimos días (Buenos Aires: ACES, 2003), p.65

27. Ellen Gould White, "Life Sketches of Ellen G. White", 1915, p. 196.2.

Chapter 8 - Modern Samarians

1. Acts 1:8

2. Acts 8:1

3. Daniel 9:24

4. John 4: 4-42; Luke 10:1 - 16

5. Ellen Gould White, "The Desire of Ages", 1898, p. 488.6.

6. Acts 8: 4,8

7. Acts 11:1 - 3

8. Acts 11:19

9. DRAE, vigésima segunda edición (2001)

10. Dennis Coon, Fundamentos de Psicología (México, D. F.: Thomson, 2005) 10 Edic., p. 517

11. John 1:9

12. 1 Corinthians 13:9,12

13. Luke 10:10 - 11

14. Ellen Gould White, "The Acts of the Apostles", 1911, p. 9.1.

15. Romans 10:14

16. Ellen Gould White, "Testimony Treasures Volume 3", 1949, p. 90.1.

17. Acts 11:20-21

18. Acts 11:22- 26

19. John Dybdahl, Adventist Mission in 21th Century (Hagerstown: Review and Herald Publishing Association, 1999), pp. 133

20. Ibid, p. 136

21. Acts 26:20 -22

22. Ephesians 4:11

23. Carlos Martin, La ciencia de ganar almas (México: GEMA/Doral, Florida: APIA, 2011), p. 61

24. John 17:15-18

25. Luis Naún Sáez, ¡Me series testigos! Cómo entrenar a los nuevos creyentes (Miami, FL: Editorial UNILIT, 1999), p. 23

26. Philip G. Samaan, El método de Cristo para testificar (Florida: APIA, 1990), p. 33

27. Sigve Tonstad, One on one with the Woman of Samaria, in http://www.ted-adventist.org/epc/presentations (Accessed on December 20, 2012)

28. Acts 10:34,35

Section IV
The challenges of urban evangelization

Chapter 9 - Running with the Horsemen

1. Ephesians 6:12

2. Exodus 14:14

3. Exodus 14:15

4. Judges 7: 16,19

5. Ellen Gould White, "Patriarchs and Prophets", 1890, p. 550.2.

6. Judges 6: 25, 26

7. Joshua 5:2,10,11

8. Ellen Gould White, "Patriarchs and Prophets", 1890, p. 255.5.

9. Exodus 4:24 - 26

10. Ellen Gould White, "Christian Service", 1925, p. 41.3.

11. Ellen Gould White, "Welfare Ministry", 1952, p. 96.1.

12. Joel Barker, Paradigma, in clubensayos.com/Temas.../Paradigma-Joel.../509754.html (Accessed on January 10, 2013)

13. Ellen Gould White, "Christian Service", 1925, p. 259.5.

14. Jeremiah 12:5

15. Lionel Matthews, Sociology: A seven day Adventist approach for students and teachers (Berrien Springs Michigan: Andrews University Press, 2006) p. 4

16. Rut Vieytes: Campos de Aplicación y Decisiones de diseño en la investigación cualitativa en Aldo Merlino: Investigación Cualitativa en Ciencias Sociales. (Buenos Aires: CENGAGE Learning, 2009) p. 56

17. John R. Weeks: Population: An introduction to concepts and issues (EEUU. Wadsworth Cengage Learning, 2012), 11 edition, p. 17

18. Romans 10:17

19. Manual de planificación estratégica Universidad de Chile in http://guiametodologica.dbe.uchile.cl/documentacion/planificacion_estrategica.pdf (Accessed on August 15, 2012)

20. Iglesia Adventista del Séptimo Día, Declaraciones, orientaciones y otros documentos (México: GEMA/Doral, Florida: APIA, 2011), p. 79

21. O C. Ferrell & Michael D. Hartline et ali, Estrategia de marketing (México, Thompson, 2006) 3era Edic., p. 28

22. Brad Powell, Cambia tu iglesia para bien (Nashville, Tennessee, Grupo Nelson, 2010)

23. Proverbs 11:14

24. Alberto M. Vallvé & Patricia Debeljuh, Misión y valores. La Empresa en busca de sentido (Buenos Aires: Gestión 2000, 2006), p. 16

25. Proverbs 11:14

26. Jairo Amaya, Gerencia, planeación y estrategia (Bucaramanga: Universidad Santo Tomás, s/d), p. 44

27. Díaz de Santos, El diagnóstico de la empresa (Madrid: MAPCAL, 1995), p. 38

28. Fred R. David, Conceptos de administración estratégica (México, Pearson Educación, 2003), p. 200

29. Revelation 19:11

Chapter 10 - Flying Through the Sky

1. http://www.aviafor.com/casos/reforestacion.htm (Accessed in July 26, 2012)

2. Ellen Gould White, "Last Day Events", 1992, p. 214.2.

3. C. Mervyn Maxwell, El destino del planeta en rebelión (Miami, Florida: APIA, 1993) 2da Edic., pp. 359 - 360

4. George R. Knight, Nuestra organización. Momentos históricos decisivos. (Florida: APIA/ México: GEMA, 2007), p. 18

5. Ellen Gould White, "Christian Experience and Teachings of Ellen G. White", 1922, p. 128.2.

6. http://www.portaladventista.org/esp/editoras (Accessed on July 26, 2012)

7. Joseph Barrett, El púlpito de Dios para la humanidad, Revista Avanzad, No. 2, Abril – Junio de 2010

8. Ellen Gould White, "Christian Experience and Teachings of Ellen G. White", 1922, p. 225.4.

9. Ellen Gould White, "Counsels on Health", 1923, p. 466.2.

10. Adventist World Radio

11. Just three years after the first radio broadcast in the United States

12. Adventistworldradio.org (Accessed on 15-8-12)

13. I Thank Dowell Chow, president of Adventist World Radio at the time of publishing this book for valuable information.

14. Milton Peverini García, Vida de Braulio Pérez Marcio (Idaho, Pacific Press Publishing Association, 2007), p. 62

15. World map of social network, en http://vincos.it/world-map-of-social-networks/ (Accessed on October 28, 2014)

16. Univisión Noticias en http://noticias.univision.com/tecnologia/redes-sociales/article/2012-04-24/facebook-llego-a-900-millones#axzz2LB70TJfx (Accessed on January 17, 2013)

17. Juan Vicente Boo, en http://www.abc.es/medios-redes/20121212/abci-twitter-papa-benedicto-tuit-201212120936.html (Accessed on January 17, 2012)

18. Diccionario de marketing (España, Cultural S.A., 1999), p. 283.

19/ Joaquín Sánchez & Teresa Pintado, Imagen Corporativa: Influencia en la gestión empresarial (Madrid: ESIC EDITORIAL,2009)

20. Paul Capriotti, planificación estratégica de la imagen corporativa (Barcelona: Editorial Ariel, 2008)

21. General Conference of Seventh-day Adventist, Global Identity Standards Manual (Silver Spring: A People of Hope Production, 1996), p. 7

Chapter 11 - The Foundation for Christian Effort

1. Aerial Warefare in http://en.wikipedia.org/wiki/Aerial_war

2. Ephesians 6:15

3. Romans 16:20

4. Ellen Gould White, "Testimonies for the Church Volume 7", 1902, p. 21.4.

5. Ellen Gould White, "Gospel Workers 1915", 1915, p. 345.1.

6. Ellen Gould White, "Testimonies for the Church Volume 9", 1909, p. 145.1.

7. Ellen Gould White, "The Review and Herald", September 30, 1902, p. 16.

8. Ellen Gould White, "The Review and Herald", 1851, p. 20.

9. Ellen Gould White, "A Call to Medical Evangelism and Health Education", 1933, p. 13.4.

10. 1 Corinthians 3:11-15

11. Ellen Gould White, "Welfare Ministry", 1952, p. 59.1.

12. Ellen Gould White, "Gospel Workers 1915", 1915, p. 468.1.

13. Ellen Gould White, "Christ's Object Lessons", 1900, p. 229.1.

14. Ellen Gould White, "The Ministry of Healing", 1905, p. 143.3.

15. Ellen Gould White, "The Review and Herald", 1851, p. 1.

16. Given the number of references in this particular section they will be placed next to the statement.

Chapter 12 - With Such an Army

1. Numbers 14:28

2. 1 Timothy 1:2; Titus 1:4

3. Ellen G. White, "A Call to Stand Apart", p.66, par.6

4. Ellen G. White, "Signs of the Times", November 3, 1881, par.21

5. Johanna Mellor & Helen Rehr, Baby Boomers. Can my eights be like my fifties? (New York: Springer Publishing Company, Inc, 2005)

6. http://www.alliancetrends.org/demographics-population.cfm?id=34 (Accessed in August 23, 2012)

7. Generation Y at http://en.wikipedia.org/wiki/Generation_Y

8. In Spanish the baton is conveniently called witness.

9. 1 Timothy 4:15

10. John Stott, Los Desafíos del Liderazgo Cristiano, (Ediciones Certeza, Buenos Aires, 2002), p. 58

11. Ellen G. White, "Counsels to Parents", Teachers and Students, p.508

12. Ellen G. White, "Messages to Young People", p.220

13. Leviticus 19:32

14. 1 John 2:14

15. Exodus 32:17,18

16. Titus 1:5

17. 1 Timothy 4:12

18. Congreso Urbano de Scupe, en Andrew Davey, Cristianismo Urbano y Globalización (London, Editorial SAL TERRAE, 2001), p. 26

19. Ellen G. White, "The Great Controversy 1888", p.365

20. Ellen G. White, "The Great Controversy 1888", pp.366,367

Chapter 13 - The Upper Class and Special Groups

1. See Wikipedia, Upper class

2. (IDEM)

3. Talcott Parsons, Un enfoque analítico de la teoría de la estratificación social, in Ensayos de teoría sociológica, (Buenos Aires, Paidós, 1967), p. 62.

4. Manuel Mora y Araujo, La estructura social de la Argentina: Evidencias y conjeturas acerca de la estratificación actual, CEPAL,Serie Políticas Sociales, N° 59, 2002.

5. Alejandro Portes y Kelly Hoffman, Las estructuras de clases en América Latina: Composición y cambios durante la época neoliberal (Santiago de Chile: CEPAL, 2003), p. 68

6. Camilo Sembler R. Estratificación social y clases sociales. Una revisión analítica de los sectores medios. (Chile: CEPAL, 2006), p. 42

7. Pierre Bourdieu, Condición de clase y posición de clase, in Estructuralismo y Sociología, Buenos Aires: Nueva Visión, 1969).

8. Ellen Gould White, "The Desire of Ages", 1898, p. 552.4.

9. Luke 19.

10. Romans 3:23, 24

11. Ephesians 2:8

12. Also a gift from God.

13. See Romans 10:17

14. John 5:39

15. Romans 10:14

16. 2 Corinthians 5:20

17. Acts 8:30 -31

18. Matthew 19:23

19. Matthew 19: 26

20. Not exclusive to them.

21. Matthew 13:22

22. Matthew 6:24

23. Matthew 19:16 -22

24. See John 3

25. Elena G. de White, Testimonios Para los Ministros (ACES: Buenos Aires, 1977) pp. 367, 368

26. 2 Kings 5:14 - 19

27. John 19:38

28. Mark 15:43

29. John 7:50

30. Isaiah 6:8

31. Revelation 14:6

32. 1 Corinthians 1:26-28

33. 2 Kings 5: 2 - 4

34. Ellen Gould White, "Prophets and Kings", 1917, p. 244.2.

35. República Dominicana

36. Nehemiah 1:11

37. Elena G. de White, Conflicto y Valor (Buenos Aires: Casa Editora Sudamericana, 1971), p. 262

38. Acts 16:31

39. Mark 5:19

40. Luke 15:5-6

41. Theory first proposed in 1930 by the Hungarian writer Frigyes Karinthy and pub-

lished in the book 'Six Degrees: The Science of a Connected Age' sociologist Duncan Watts. Ensures that one can access anyone on the planet in just six "steps."

42. Ellen Gould White, "Welfare Ministry", 1952, p. 280.3.

43. Ellen Gould White, "Counsels on Diet and Foods", 1938, p. 207.5.

44. Ellen Gould White, "The Acts of the Apostles", 1911, p. 140.1.

45. Ellen Gould White, "Christian Service", 1925, p. 203.3.

46. Ellen Gould White, "The Ministry of Healing", 1905, p. 213.5.

47. Ellen Gould White, "Evangelism", 1946, p. 556.4.

48. IDEM

49. Ellen Gould White, "The Acts of the Apostles", 1911, p. 140.1.

50. Ansel Oliver, Adventist News Network, in http://news.adventist.org/es/archive/articles/2010/02/23/founder-of-adventist-deaf-ministry-dies-at-89. (Accessed on February 25, 2013)

Section V
Success in Urban Evangelism

Chapter 14 - Cities of Refuge

1. Joshua 20:1 - 4

2. Deuteronomy 19:1 -2

3. See Deuteronomy 19:3, 6, 9

4. See Deuteronomy 4:41

5. Comentario bíblico adventista del séptimo día (California: Pacific Press, 1978, t.1), p. 983

6. Deuteronomy 4:42; Exodus 21:13;Deuteronony 19: 4 -5

7. IDEM

8. Numbers 35:6, 7

9. Numbers 35: 12 -15

10. Numbers 35: 16 - 24

11. Numbers 35:25-28

12. Numbers 35:32

13 Joshua 20:4 -9

14. Deuteronomy 19:11 - 13

15. Quoted by Stephen N. Haskell, La sombre de la cruz (Florida: APIA/ México: GEMA,2011) p. 241

16. Ellen G. White, Patriarcs and Prophets, pp.515,516

17. Matthew 11:28

18. Isaiah 56:7 and Mark 11:17

19. Ellen G. White, The Acts of the Apostles, p.11

20. John 13:35

21. 1 Corinthians 13:2

22. Ellen Gould White, "Welfare Ministry", 1952, p. 86.2.

23. John 17:20-21

24. Ellen G. White, Testimonies for the Church, vol.9, p.221, par.1

25. Ellen G. White, Testimonies for the Church, vol.8, p.242, par.1

26. Ellen G. White, Letter 110, 1893

27. Acts 2:44; Acts 4:32-34

28. Romans 15:4

29. Isaiah 58: 6- 8

30. James 1:27

31. Ellen G. White, The Desire of Ages, p.141, par.5

32. Ellen G. White, Testimonies for the Church, p.491, par.1

33. Christian A. Schwarz, Desarrollo Natural de la Iglesia (Barcelona: Clie, 1996) p. 31

34. 1 Corinthians 14:40

35. Pedrito U. Maynard – Reid, Complete Evangelism (Scottdale: Herald Press, 1997) p. 7

36. Ellen G. White, The Ministry of Healing, p.143, par.3

37. Matthew 14:14-16

38. Acts 6:1-6

39. Ellen G. White, RH March 4, 1902

40. Acts 2:44-45

41. Acts 3:1-6

42. Dan Buettner, Los secretos de una vida larga, noviembre de 2005, en http://www.abo.org.ar/web/NationalGeographicAdv.htm (Accessed on February 27, 2013)

43. Ellen G. White, RH Hune 25, 1959

44. Ellen G. White, Manuscrito 114, 1902

45. Ellen G. White, Testimonies for the Church, vol.9, p.112

46. Ellen G. White, Testimonies for the Church, vol.7, p.95

47. Ellen G. White, Testimonies for the Church, vol.9, p.167

48. Ellen G. White, The Ministry of Healing, pp.125,126

49. Larry Burkett, Curso de Liderazgo Económico (Colombia: Conceptos Financieros Crown, 2006), p. 21

50. G. Edward Reid, Fe y Finanzas (EEUU: S/N, 2009), p. 8

51. Matthew 6:24

52. Larry Burkett, Usando su dinero sabiamente (Miami, Florida: Editorial Unilit, 1996), p. 36

53. See Exodus 25:8, 2 Chronicles 7:12 and Mark 11:17

54. Ellen G. White, Letter 168, 1909

Chapter 15 - Not by Power, but by My Spirit

1. Zachary 4: 6

2. Diccionario Bíblico Adventista, p. 1224

3. Comentario Bíblico Adventista del Séptimo Día (Boise, Idaho: Pacific Press, 1985, t.4), p. 1116

4. John 16: 13

5. Acts 2:47

6. Ephesians 4: 11- 12

7. Acts 8:29,30

8. Acts 13:2

9. 1 Chorintians 3:6

10. Ron E. M. Clouzet, Adventism´s greatest need. The Outpouring of the Holy Spirit (Nampa, Idaho, Pacific Press, 2011), p. 178

11. Ellen Gould White, "Patriarchs and Prophets", 1890, p. 509.1.

12. Ellen Gould White, "Counsels on Stewardship", 1940, p. 40.2.

13. Elena G. de White, Consejos sobre mayordomía cristiana (México: GEMA/Doral, Florida: APIA, 2005), p. 39

14. Psalm 24:1-2

15. Elena G. de White, Recibiréis poder (Buenos Aires: Casa Editora Sudamericana, 2009). p. 177

16. Ellen Gould White, "Evangelism", 1946, p. 87.1.

17. Ellen Gould White, "Evangelism", 1946, p. 88.1.

18. See Revelation 17: 1 - 6

19. See Matthew 9:17

20. Acts 1:8

21. Adventist Hymnal, no. 260